T0386672

# VIETNAMESE VEGETARIAN

# VIETNAMESE VEGETARIAN

SIMPLE VEGETARIAN
RECIPES FROM A VIETNAMESE
HOME KITCHEN

Uyen Luu

Hardie Grant
BOOKS

Introduction 7
I am not a Vegetarian 10
Vegetarian Vietnamese 10
How to Use this Book 11
Essential Ingredients 12
Kitchen Tips, Must-Haves 15

Chapter 1

PLAYFUL EATING: SNACKS AND MORE 16

Chapter 2

RICE IS LIFE: AND WHAT TO EAT WITH IT 36

Chapter 3

SALAD DAYS 72

Chapter 4

ONE-PLATE NOODLES 90

Midweek Menu 215
Weekend Feasting Menu 216
Dinner Party Menu 217
About the Author 218
Acknowledgements 219
Index 220

Chapter 5

CRAVINGS 112

Chapter 6

SOUPS FOR THE SOUL 138

Chapter 7

SWEET TREATS 160

Chapter 8

LITTLE THINGS 188

# INTRODUCTION



'I have the most delicious bunch of fragrant Thai basil,' says my mother. 'Shall I make a pot of phở?' We are not vegetarian but I have been brought up to love my vegetables. Growing up, my mum featured all our meals around herbs, fruit and vegetables. We will have fried fish because tomatoes are in season, along with tofu and grilled aubergines. In a meal, we would have about three or four vegetarian dishes and one protein dish, shared together with rice.

Family meals or eating together is hugely paramount in the Vietnamese culture. Casual talk about the food you've enjoyed or about to delight in is popular chit-chat. That small talk embarks on all sorts of meaning and affiliations as true feelings are rarely spoken.

My mum sings, when she talks about food. Fruit and vegetables make her very excited and you can tell her level of happiness by the way she cooks, eats and talks about food. The intonations of the Vietnamese language convey as much meaning, spirit and emotion as the words, and so my mother's excited yells also chirped about steaming purple sweet potatoes, and shrieked about fragrant, juicy limes in dipping sauces, as if every season presents her with a new surprise or a memory of a good thing coming back to life.

'My neighbour told me that Chinese violets are in season,' she would whisper, 'they are really great for a good night's sleep', as if the secret violets would sell out, if she spoke any louder. 'I have found some,' she would say in a more daring voice. 'Shall I make a soup or shall I fry it with garlic?' In the next triumphant breath, she pulls a green, almost yellowing mango out of her shopping bag and breathes it in. 'This is a gift for Olive [my daughter]. Smell it, go on, smell it....' Victorious, she would chant, *'Ngon quá trời ngon!'* (So delicious, heavenly delicious.)

My mum and her friends were the only Vietnamese people I knew growing up in London. All I know, I know by eavesdropping on their kitchen talk while they laboured me on dumpling-folding duties and rolling spring rolls. They have been a sisterhood – a clan of women who support each other's wellbeing, sing karaoke, jiggle a dance together, share food, endlessly discuss recipes and techniques and natter about herbs, fruit and vegetables – since the early 1980s. It is as if the plants in which they speak reflect the sweetness of life, the sourness it brings, the bitterness it embeds and the spiciness it embraces. The beauty and deliciousness of their dishes mirror the compassion and affection that are often suppressed inside them.

Unsurprisingly, my mum's life revolves around food. The conversation only ever starts with, 'Have you eaten yet?' To cook well is to exhibit your love, kindness, friendship and compassion that you express through the colours, the flavours and the vibrancy in your cooking.

The secret to good Vietnamese cooking is: herbs and vegetables that elevate a dish. The perfect balance of contrasting sweet, sour, hot, umami and bitter flavours harmonises with different textures and temperatures. This is what makes Vietnamese a brilliant cuisine and one of the most delicious. Whilst, the colour entices, and brings joy and pleasure.

Imagine the exhilaration when my mum first found coriander (cilantro) in London; they threw a carpet picnic of summer rolls and celebrated with full mic karaoke, volume 11. And when a friend discovered that they sold fresh pandan leaves in Chinatown, they threw everyone's birthday parties. And when supermarkets started to stock honeyed mango and green papaya, the parties got more and more elaborate.

Having grown up in Britain, I was often torn between the two sides of my identity. One which was rich with steamed pandan-flavoured desserts and one with paper bags of battered haddock and salty, vinegary soggy chips (French fries). Never knowing if I was Vietnamese or British or how to combine the two, I resented my mother's cooking as a teenager because it was not what everyone else was eating. But at the same time, how I loved it.

In the urbanscape of damp and drizzly Hackney, the smells of star anise and black cardamon lingered two streets down, and a bowl of steaming-hot, delicious noodles greeted me home. She tore the leaves of Thai basil onto my phở which transformed the charred onion and ginger broth to another level. She squeezed every last drop of the first fresh lime she got hold of since we left Vietnam. The exquisite scent brought back homesick memories of my grandmothers and aunties who would often serve me ice-cold lime sodas with strawberry syrup (page 186). They even rubbed their hands and conditioned their hair with the leftover rind of limes. Nothing ever went to waste.

On busier days when she had too much to do, I would smell that delicious, buttery, garlicky egg-fried rice, peppered with golden sweetcorn and green peas, using up leftover rice and freezer goods. It is the flavour of home and the flavour of her love.

On weekends when my friends came for sleepovers or if it was my birthday party, a bounty of crispy and perfectly uniform spring rolls and bright yellow coconut crêpes lined a buffet. My childhood memories are filled with the glorious food my mother made, and as a cook, I am constantly wanting to achieve the characteristics of her cooking – a mix of instinct and practise; often fast, frugal and perfectly balanced. I have used her principles to write recipes in this book, adapting many favourite Vietnamese dishes to vegetarian and layering on flavour after flavour as she has taught me to do. It was always her food which helped me to find my way through the weathers of life and my path back home.

# I AM NOT A VEGETARIAN

I am a feeder, I am an eater, I am an omnivore. I love eating plants. Like many in recent times, I try to cut down on meat and try to buy from responsible and sustainable sources where possible. I am a part-time vegetarian, not only trying to make a difference but because I enjoy it. In a typical meal, I would make a handful of vegetarian dishes, or I would use at least four different plants to surround a bowl.

I would happily serve a whole feast with only vegetarian and vegan dishes on my Vietnamese menu. I prefer a lot of traditional recipes without the meat or excessive amounts of seafood. I loved spending the time that I did writing these recipes; I felt the opportunities to eat plants in the most delicious ways were endless.

# VEGETARIAN VIETNAMESE

The presence of fruit, vegetables, herbs and legumes are integral and deeply rooted in mainstream Vietnamese cooking. On a typical Vietnamese table, plants are highly featured and there are many exciting vegetable dishes that are part of a balanced meal. They are not considered optional or sides, but play an important, must-have role in every meal. Tofu isn't considered a replacement for meat or fish but is enjoyed entirely for itself. Vegetarian dishes aren't consumed under the guise of needing five-a-day; they are enjoyed purely as vegetables.

Although being 100 per cent vegetarian for health, ethnical or environmental reasons is a recent thing, a lot of Vietnamese people are already part-time vegetarians, as Buddhism is part of the Vietnamese culture, and many take on a vegetarian diet monthly or every now and again to practise mindfulness and kindness. Every beat of a butterfly wing, and so on...

Just say *ăn chay* (eat vegetarian) and this is respected by the family and the surrounding community. But as a nation of people who love their fish and meat, the fear of missing out is ultimately huge, therefore there are always vegetarian versions of much-loved meaty favourites such as phở, because no one can live without it. No one. Not even the monks.

This book focuses on making heroes of vegetables in some vegetarian versions of favourite Vietnamese dishes. You can use two to three of these recipes to add to a meal with fried fish, for example. They can be enjoyed as midweek meals, weekend treats or feast gatherings. As well as ease and simplicity, my focus is on flavour, texture and balance so that each dish can be valued as enjoyable vegetarian dishes in their own right and even the biggest carnivores won't feel as if they are missing out.

Although it is not always possible to have a wide variety of Vietnamese herbs and vegetables at our disposal, there are plenty of ways to use ingredients that are readily available and still enjoy Vietnamese food as it should be enjoyed. Refreshing and umami flavours are present in herbs and vegetables, layered with notes from storecupboard condiments, spices and ferments to replicate typical and traditional dishes.

# HOW TO USE THIS BOOK

I love cooking, I love creating recipes and here I gave myself a chance to be very creative in the kitchen to meet the Vietnamese flavour profiles, as well as considering balanced textures. Although I would never sacrifice deliciousness, I am a simple cook and I like to get dinner done without a fuss. I often enjoy looking in my storecupboard and (sometimes bare) refrigerator to see what tasty dish I can come up with.

It is really important to understand the flavours of your condiments and storecupboard ingredients. Some are saltier, sharper or sweeter than what I have used; always taste your seasoning and adjust the balance. If a seasoning or other ingredient isn't available, try using something similar and, to help you, I've listed alternatives throughout.

When I ask for vegan fish sauce, feel free to use fish sauce if your ethics are similar to mine. If you don't have vegan fish sauce or vegetable umami seasoning, use soy sauce. If you don't have limes, use lemon or vinegar.

You may notice though that some recipes have quite a long list of ingredients, but don't be intimidated; the steps are usually simple or it all goes into one pan. Some dishes need the layering of flavours and some thrive on being modest.

Most recipes start with a small round shallot or two. I love these, especially the pink Asian variety. A little shallot goes a long way and flavours every dish beautifully. If you can't get the pink ones, the brown ones are good too. Avoid using big shallots unless specified or only use a little of a large one. If you can't get any shallots, use onion. Many recipes also start with garlic; don't be shy.

Unless specified, I use a cold-pressed rapeseed (canola) oil for most of my cooking but, sometimes, a neutral cooking oil like sunflower (safflower) oil is good because it is flavourless; other oils carry a lot of their own flavours which could affect the overall smell and taste of a dish.

I recommend first following the recipes to have a feel for the balanced flavours and textures, before playing around with them. I am aware that not everything is always readily available, and I believe that you can create your own delicious dishes using this book as a guide.

Before making a dish, check the ingredients list, read through the method and prep and organise your worktop in order of use. While waiting for certain parts to cook, see if you can carry on prepping for later stages to save on time.

I have estimated and round off timings for preparation and cooking times to give you a rough guidance on how long it takes to achieve a recipe.

I have used ingredients that feel fitting to the flavour profiles, which hopefully pair well together, but feel free to substitute herbs and vegetables; use what you have available. Always taste, taste and taste as you go to gift yourself the perfect balance of flavours.

# ESSENTIAL INGREDIENTS

I like to keep my storecupboard fully stocked with essential ingredients that layer flavour upon flavour and season my cooking, giving it more depth; its unique Vietnamese identity, combining tradition with modernity.

The little jars and bottles act as both building blocks and accessories to my recipes. If you can afford to experiment with different brands and types, then the foundation of your cooking will get stronger and better as you cook more and more.

There are certain things that we can make at home and maximise on freshness, like spending an hour brewing a homemade stock to satisfy the week's needs and cravings, and save cooking time down the line. I like toasting my own sesame seeds because nothing beats the fragrance of it coming straight from the hot pan, or I will fry a bunch of shallots for crispy touches to any dishes. I love making my own Lemongrass and Chilli Oil too (page 210) to finish a dish off or infuse a Homemade Vegan Fish Sauce (page 193). There is truly nothing better than making things yourself when you have time and the resources to do so.

However, there are some great products out there that add lots of flavour. These are are my essential basics:

- Maldon salt
- Maggi soy sauce
- Yondu vegetable umami sauce
- mushroom vegetarian oyster sauce
- Laoganma crispy chilli oil
- maple syrup
- Aspall cider vinegar
- coconut water
- coconut milk
- jasmine rice
- a variety of noodles

MUSHROOM
VEGETARIAN
SAVOY
Pandan
USDA ORGANIC
Cypressa
300g
Epicure
Farrington's
BRITISH
340g
BLACK BEAN RĀYU

## STORECUPBOARD INGREDIENTS

### Salty/Umami

Vietnamese Maggi soy sauce (this is the one used throughout this book and is closest to Chinese-style light soy sauce), vegetarian oyster sauce, mushroom seasoning powder, nutritional yeast, fermented tofu, miso, black bean sauce, Marmite, perilla sauce, spicy bean sauce, crispy chilli oil, Maggi liquid seasoning, vegetable umami sauce, vegan fish sauce

### Sweet

Caster (superfine) sugar, maple syrup, agave syrup, honey, coconut sugar, palm sugar, rock sugar, date syrup, mirin, sweet chilli sauce

### Sour

Cider vinegar, rice wine vinegar, white wine vinegar, black vinegar, ponzu, yuzu

### Bitter

Mustard, sake, ponzu

### Spicy

Chilli sauces, chilli oils, chilli powder, chilli (hot pepper) flakes

Vietnamese families include children in all their meals and therefore have spicy condiments to add to their own bowls. In these recipes, I have mainly specified chillies as optional.

## HERBS AND AROMATICS

When making a vermicelli noodle salad bowl or cooking recipes with salad wraps, it is customary to have a good selection of fragrant leaves which add heaps of flavour and texture to every bite.

To keep most herbs fresh, de-stalk or leave whole, but do give them a good soak in a bowl of water for 30–60 minutes. Wash and dry them in a salad spinner. If you do not have a salad spinner, flick the water off them and rest on a clean tea towel (dish towel) to completely dry out, turning occasionally. Store in an airtight container in the refrigerator.

Thai basil is the exception; keep it intact with the stem. It is best to wash it only minutes before using.

### Herbs

Vietnamese coriander (laksa leaf), Vietnamese balm, perilla, sawtooth (Thai parsley), Thai basil, garlic chives, fish mint, betel leaves (cooked), garden mint, mugwort leaves, Vietnamese balm

### Aromatics

Lemongrass, fresh ginger root, shallots, garlic

## USE OF NON-VEGETARIAN PRODUCTS

As I am not a vegetarian myself, I do use fish sauce in my cooking, simply because it touches base with all the tastebuds and I love it. Fish sauce is the staple of Vietnamese cooking and premium fish sauce truly makes everything taste wonderful, so if you're like me – not a true vegetarian – use fish sauce if you prefer.

In these recipes I suggest using Homemade Vegetable Stock (page 196) or vegetable stock cubes, mushroom seasoning powder or vegetarian oyster sauce, but if you have fresh chicken stock going, use that, as this is what I do. I am a strong believer in using what you have available (according to your ethics) and so reducing waste and further consumption. Use your instinct and tastebuds if you need to replace or substitute an ingredient.

Sometimes, I use ghee, eggs and honey; feel free to substitute these for vegan alternatives or omit.

# KITCHEN TIPS, MUST-HAVES

It is always good to be well organised, including your worktop; have your ingredients to use on one side and place used ones to be put away on another. Prep is key. Clean up after yourself as you go.

- Make prep easy by investing in a good chef's knife, a serrated knife, kitchen scissors (good to help save on some washing-up) and a couple of cutting boards – I have one large wooden one so I can set aside prepped vegetables as I go.
- Compost food waste. Peelings, odds and ends can be used to make vegetable stock, then you can strain and compost them.
- Invest in glass Tupperware of different sizes to store prepped ingredients and leftovers; as they have lids, there is no need to use cling film (plastic wrap). I save all my jars and try to reuse plastic containers and recycle them when broken.
- To make life easy, these are the utensils I find most useful: cooking chopsticks, a spider, wooden cooking spatula, silicone spatula, ladle, large utility spoon, tongs, colanders, thermometer, vegetable peeler, Vietnamese julienne grater, a small and large measuring jug.
- In my cooking, I need a well-seasoned wok, a small range of pots and pans with lids, a bamboo steamer and a casserole dish (Dutch oven).
- If rice is often on the menu, a rice cooker is a must. My Instant Pot cooks rice amongst other things for quick energy-saving tactics. I reheat leftover food in a microwave.
- A kettle speeds up cooking time or use a lid when boiling water.
- A clock or kitchen timer (you can use one on your phone) is great to keep you from over- or underdoing the cooking.

# PLAYFUL EATING:

ONE

# SNACKS AND MORE

Eating together is at the heart of Vietnamese culture and *ăn chơi* (playful or joyful eating) is considered being kind to yourself by giving yourself and others a fun gift of food. The Vietnamese believe that such playful eating strengthens closeness and connection to each other, which therefore brings harmony and compassion to relationships. This covers a whole range of foods, not just snacks.

I love hosting an afternoon of weekend feasting, with my friends helping me fold dumplings and chop vegetables. Getting friends to help in the kitchen is another way to bring us even closer together. My mum will usually have her friends pull herb leaves off their stems or cut out dumpling pastry shapes, while others gather in another room (with previously made snacks) and sing with animation into the karaoke microphones, intense in their sentiment and sincerity. The music is loud; they like the tunes to engulf them. In Vietnam, you get music blasting from speakers, even on trains and buses. It's the same with food; the overwhelming need for instant gratification and satisfaction.

When travelling, my mum would always pack a case or bag full of food. Sticky rice wrapped in banana leaf, dumplings, summer rolls, bánh mì and always a cold noodle salad or fried rice. To lack these provisions would be *rất buồn* (very sad) which is a feeling that always needs eradicating. Sometimes when we arrived at a beautiful, peaceful, green countryside, she would say, *'đẹp...'* (beautiful) and then *'có vẻ cô đơn'* (seems lonely) and we'd end up travelling back home where more food awaits.

My family in Vietnam love to be with others and it seems to me their whole existence depends on gathering and eating; therefore they always indulge in *ăn chơi* – eating for fun.

I first discovered the true meaning and power of *ăn chơi* during my art-school days at Central Saint Martin's in Soho, in the late 90s. I gathered my ravenous fellow students for a brisk walk to a café in Chinatown serving cheap rice meals. It was so good and so fun! We sealed our bond over blanched choi sum and free jasmine tea. With my Saturday job money, I would arrive to classes with golden milk buns filled with coconut custard and pandan sponge cakes. In sharing these snacks, we built friendships that are still true and lasting to this day.

# CABBAGE, TOFU AND KIMCHI DUMPLINGS

HÁ CẢO CHAY

I love vegetables to retain some bite, which is why I like to use a knife to chop and slice them, but you can also pulse up leftover roasted vegetables with shallots, garlic and ginger and stir in the tofu. These dumplings can be shallow-fried, deep-fried, steamed or poached. Freeze them to enjoy in the future; cook from frozen.

Makes approx. 25
Prep time — 35 minutes
Cooking time — 20–30 minutes

For the seasoning

1 tablespoon soy sauce
1 teaspoon agave syrup
1 teaspoon ponzu or cider vinegar
1 tablespoon rice wine or Shaoxing wine or sherry

For the filling

1 tablespoon ghee or vegetable oil
1 shallot, finely chopped
2 garlic cloves, crushed
2.5 cm (1 in) fresh ginger root, finely chopped
30 g (1 oz) cabbage, shredded or thinly sliced
30 g (1 oz) asparagus, sliced into 5 mm (¼ in) rings
30 g (1 oz) fresh or frozen garden peas (thawed) or edamame beans
190 g (6⅔ oz) medium-firm tofu, pressed, mashed
100 g (3½ oz) kimchi, coarsely chopped
pinch of white pepper
½ teaspoon mushroom seasoning powder

For the shallow-frying

1 tablespoon cornflour (cornstarch)
1 pack of 25 Japanese gyoza or wonton wrappers (thaw if from frozen) or Dumpling Wrappers (page 195)
2 tablespoons cooking oil
150 ml (5 fl oz/scant ⅔ cup) boiling water

Dipping sauce options (page 212)

shiso dressing
soy sauce and ponzu
soy sauce and yuzu mustard

In a small bowl, mix the seasoning ingredients together. Set aside.

In a frying pan (skillet), add the ghee over a medium heat and fry the shallot until slightly golden, then add the garlic and ginger to cook for a couple of minutes. Throw in the cabbage, asparagus, peas, mashed tofu and kimchi. Season with white pepper, mushroom seasoning powder and the seasoning mix. Cook for about 5 minutes then set aside to cool before squeezing out and discarding all the juices.

Prepare a tray to place your dumplings. Sprinkle it with the cornflour. Take a dumpling wrapper, moisten half of one edge with a touch of water, place a teaspoon of filling in the middle, fold the wrapper in half, pushing out any air, to create a half moon, then pinch the sides and hem together every 5 mm (¼ in). You should get between 5–7 pleats. Place the dumplings on the tray, using your fingers to push the bottom down to create a flat bottom. Repeat until done.

In a frying pan, bring the oil to a medium heat and place the dumplings side by side in the pan with 1 cm (½ in) between them. Cook with a lid on for 5 minutes. Then add the boiling water from the kettle and continue to cook with the lid on for about 5 minutes until the water has completely evaporated, before removing the lid and frying the dumplings for another 3–5 minutes until the bottoms are golden.

Alternatively, deep-fry the dumplings in 2.5 cm (1 in) oil at 140°C (275°F) for 5 minutes or until golden, crispy and bubbly.

Serve warm with a dipping sauce of choice. If you can't wait, a splash of good quality soy sauce and some sriracha will do just fine!

NOTE

These are great in a hot broth or noodle soup. You can use any vegetables you may have lying around: tinned water chestnuts, frozen vegetables like sweetcorn, pumpkin, Jerusalem artichokes, etc. Make sure you squeeze out any liquid from the filling.

# ROASTED CAULIFLOWER AND AUBERGINE DUMPLINGS

HÁ CẢO NHÂN CÀ TÍM VÀ BÔNG CẢI TRẮNG

I love getting creative with dumpling fillings; there are so many possibilities. Here, I've added my favourite roasted vegetables together, along with a moreish tang and spice of shop-bought or homemade (page 207) pickled mustard greens or kimchi. To make a more substantial meal, I enjoy these on a bed of seasonal greens, such as monk's beard (pictured) or samphire, which have been simply pan-fried with garlic and ginger. This filling can be used with wonton wrappers too. The dumplings can be fried, steamed or poached.

Makes approx. 25
Prep time — 35 minutes
Cooking time — 45 minutes

¼ cauliflower, sliced into 1 cm (½ in) florets
130 g (4½ oz) aubergine (eggplant)
3½ tablespoons neutral cooking oil
pinch of sea salt
60 g (2 oz) leek, finely sliced
10 g (⅓ oz) fresh ginger root, finely chopped
40 g (1½ oz) pickled mustard greens or kimchi, juices squeezed out, chopped into 1 cm (½ in) pieces
1 tablespoon soy sauce
2 teaspoons black vinegar
20 g (¾ oz) garlic chives, snipped into 1 cm (½ in) pieces
1 pack of 25 Japanese gyoza or wonton wrappers (thaw from frozen) or Dumpling Wrappers (page 195)
pinch of cornflour

To serve (optional)

soy sauce
crispy chilli oil
bed of watercress or lamb's lettuce
pan-fried monk's beard
pan-fried samphire
selection of dressings (page 212)

Preheat a fan oven to 200°C (400°F/gas 6). Add the cauliflower and aubergine to a baking sheet, drizzle over 1 tablespoon of the oil, season with sea salt and roast for 25 minutes. When done, scoop out the aubergine flesh from its skin (discard the skin) and chop into small pieces.

Fry the leek and ginger over a medium heat with 1 tablespoon of the oil, then add the roasted cauliflower, aubergine and mustard greens. Add the soy sauce and black vinegar and stir-fry for 4 minutes. Turn off the heat and mix in the garlic chives. Set aside in a bowl to cool to room temperature.

Fill each wrapper with a teaspoon and a bit of filling. Moisten half of one edge of the dumpling with a touch of water, fold the wrapper in half, pushing any air out, to create a half moon, then pinch the sides and hem together every 5 mm (¼ in). You should get between 5–7 pleats. While working, place the filled dumplings on a tray with a pinch of cornflour. Repeat with all the wrappers.

To pan-fry, bring a frying pan (skillet) to a medium heat, add the remaining oil and place the dumplings next to each other, 1 cm (½ in) apart. Cook for a minute then add about 5 mm (¼ in) depth of just-boiled water to the pan and cover with a lid. Let the dumplings cook until the water has evaporated and then pan-fry until you get a crispy golden bottom.

Serve on their own with soy sauce and crispy chilli oil or on a bed of flavoursome greens drenched in a variety of dressings on page 212. Also delicious as a topping on bánh canh noodle soup (page 144) or southern noodle soup (page 146).

# TAPIOCA DUMPLINGS WITH SWEET LIME



BÁNH BỘT LỌC CHAY

Inspired by the famous Phan Thiết street food speciality with prawns (shrimp), these translucent dumplings are to die for. The secret to their deliciousness is the smoothness and softness of the dumpling wrappers and the simple yet gorgeous dressing. Work the dough with great urgency with just-boiled water. If you do use fish sauce, this is the one recipe to use it in. These are great to prep ahead for dinner parties as a starter; cook when ready to serve.

Serves 2–4 as a starter
Makes 20
Prep time — 30 minutes
Cooking time — 10 minutes

For the filling

1 tablespoon vegetable oil
1 garlic clove, finely chopped
50 g (1¾ oz) carrot, cut into 5 mm (¼ in) cubes
40 g (1½ oz) cauliflower, cut into 5 mm (¼ in) cubes
40 g (1½ oz) okra, sliced into 5 mm (¼ in) discs
40 g (1½ oz) sugar snap peas, cut into 5 mm (¼ in) cubes
¼ teaspoon sea salt
¼ teaspoon sugar
½ teaspoon nutritional yeast

For the spring onion oil (page 210)

For the sweet lime sauce

juice of ½ lime
2 tablespoons sugar
2 tablespoons Yondu vegetable umami sauce, Homemade Vegan Fish Sauce (page 193) or soy sauce
1 bird's eye chilli, sliced thinly at a diagonal

For the dough

100 g (3½ oz) tapioca starch, plus 20 g (¾ oz) for dusting
65 ml (2⅕ fl oz/generous ¼ cup) boiling hot water

In a frying pan (skillet), heat the oil over a medium heat and fry the garlic until slightly golden, then add the carrot, cauliflower, okra and sugar snap peas. Season with salt, sugar and nutritional yeast. Fry for 3 minutes then set the filling aside to cool.

To make the spring onion oil, in a medium frying pan, follow the instructions on page 210 and set aside.

Combine the sweet lime sauce ingredients and divide into dipping bowls.

To make the dough, add the tapioca starch to a bowl. Using a wooden spoon, slowly stir in the just-boiled water in a circular direction until combined. Once it forms a dough, quickly knead the hot dough with your hands until it becomes a smooth ball. Roll it into a sausage and cut it in half. Slice each half into 10 pieces (12 g (scant ½ oz) each).

On a dusted board, use a rolling pin, roll out a disc of 3 mm thickness and 8 cm (3 in) diameter. Add a teaspoon of filling, fold the dough over it to create a half moon, then pinch the edges together to stick. Set aside in an airtight container and repeat with the rest of the dough and filling.

To cook, bring a saucepan of water to the boil, then gently place in enough dumplings, one by one, to fit the pan but do not crowd it. Prevent them from sticking together by separating them with a pair of chopsticks. When they float to the top at around 3 minutes, cook for a further minute and remove them from the water with a spider onto the frying pan with the spring onion oil. Coat in the oil to prevent them from sticking together.

Spread them out on a serving plate, smother them with more spring onion oil and serve immediately with the sweet lime sauce.

NOTE

The trick with the dough is to be as fast as you can. Have a wooden spoon ready to mix so, as soon as you pour just-boiled water into the flour, get mixing and then quickly get your hands kneading. Don't lose a second.

# SWEET POTATO AND WATER CHESTNUT WONTONS

HOÀNH THÁNH CHAY

There is nothing better than making a batch of wontons with a loved one and having a good old natter about everything and nothing at all. The tranquillity and comfort usually seeps into the pleats and folds. These wontons are great deep-fried, poached or steamed. They can be enjoyed with lots of sauce and a side of blanched green; they garnish delicious noodle soups as more-ish toppings.

Makes approx. 24
Prep time — 40 minutes
Cooking time — 40 minutes

For the perilla and black vinegar sauce

1½ tablespoons black vinegar
3 tablespoons perilla sauce or 2 tablespoons soy sauce
1 tablespoon maple syrup
2 teaspoons shop-bought crispy chilli oil

For the wontons

200 g (7 oz) cauliflower, broken into 1 cm (½ in) florets
300 g (10½ oz) sweet potato or pumpkin, peeled, sliced into 1 cm (½ in) pieces
1 tablespoon rapeseed (canola) oil
80 g (3 oz) edamame beans, or asparagus or green beans, sliced into 5 mm (¼ in) pieces
80 g (3 oz) water chestnuts, chopped into 5 mm (¼ in) cubes
1 tablespoon sushi ginger, finely chopped
3 spring onions (scallions), finely sliced
¾ teaspoon sea salt
1 teaspoon sesame oil
1 tablespoon cornflour (cornstarch), for dusting
1 pack of shop-bought 8 x 8 cm (3 x 3 in) wonton wrappers

For deep-frying

oil, about 5 cm (2 in) depth in a wok

For poaching

1 tablespoon sesame oil

For the garnish

spring onion (scallion), sliced

Preheat a fan oven to 200°C (400°F/gas 6).

Make the sauce by mixing the ingredients together. Set aside.

Place the cauliflower and sweet potato onto a baking tray (pan). Drizzle and toss with the oil and bake for 25–25 minutes.

When the vegetables are done, let them cool slightly before roughly mashing the sweet potato in a mixing bowl. Add the cauliflower, edamame, water chestnuts, sushi ginger and spring onions. Sprinkle with the sea salt and gently fold it altogether with the sesame oil.

To make the dumplings, sprinkle a little cornflour onto a tray. Place a wonton wrapper onto the palm of your hand and place 1 tablespoon of the filling in the middle. Fold into a triangle and roughly pleat together. Place it on the tray. This technique is great for deep-frying. If you would like to poach the wontons, pleat them into gold sacks by folding into a triangle then pinching inwards until the wrappers gather at the top, before placing the wontons on a tray. Repeat.

To deep-fry

Heat the oil to 160°C (320°F) and fry in batches for about 3 minutes on each side or until blistering and golden. Drain on paper towels.

To poach

Place in a pan of boiling water and poach in batches for 4 minutes, at which point they should float to the top. Leave to poach for another minute before draining and then gently tossing in the sesame oil.

To serve

Place on a platter and pour the perilla sauce all over it. Scatter with spring onion.

These go well with southern noodle soup (page 146), bánh canh noodle soup (page 144) or seasoned homemade vegetable stock (page 196) with herbs and spring onions.

# VEGETABLE CURRY PUFFS

BÁNH PATÊ SÔ CÀ RI CHAY

Known as *bánh patê sô* from the French *pâté chaud*, they traditionally come as a hot meat pie eaten with a beer or cup of coffee. They can easily be picked up along the traffic-filled streets of Sài Gòn but I haven't seen a curry-filled one in Vietnam, so mine is based on my love for a veggie samosa. These are great for parties, picnics, lunch boxes and snacking.

Makes 12–15
Prep time — 30 minutes
Cooking time — 45 minutes

1 tablespoon rapeseed (canola) oil
1 small round shallot, roughly chopped
2 garlic cloves, roughly sliced
1 red onion, diced
60 g (2 oz) carrot, diced into 1 cm (½ in) cubes
60 g (2 oz) potato, diced into 1 cm (½ in) cubes
60 g (2 oz) asparagus, cut into 1 cm (½ in) cubes
120 g (4 oz) cauliflower, broken into 2 cm florets
2 tablespoons Vietnamese curry powder or mild curry powder
1 tablespoon nutritional yeast
sea salt and freshly ground black pepper
handful of frozen edamame beans or frozen peas
150 ml (5 fl oz/scant ½ cup) coconut milk
1 teaspoon cornflour (cornstarch)
750 g (1 lb 10 oz) ready-made puff pastry sheets
1 egg, beaten
1 teaspoon chilli (hot pepper) flakes (optional)

Preheat a fan oven to 200°C (400°F/gas 6). Line a baking tray (pan) with baking parchment.

Over a medium-high heat, add the oil to a frying pan (skillet) with the shallot and garlic. Fry until golden, then add the red onion, carrot, potato, asparagus and cauliflower. Fry for about 5 minutes until slightly soft. Sprinkle over the curry powder, nutritional yeast, salt and pepper, then add the edamame and cook for a further 2 minutes. Stir in the coconut milk and continue to cook the filling for another 5 minutes.

In a separate bowl, mix the cornflour with 2 tablespoons of water, then pour the mixture in a circular motion into the pan of filling and stir to thicken the sauce. Cook for a further minute and leave to cool to room temperature.

Use a rolling pin to roll out the sheet of puff pastry some more. Use a 8 cm (3 in) cookie cutter to cut the pastry. Dot 2 tablespoons of filling on one side and fold over. Press a fork on the edges to seal. Repeat with the rest and brush the pastry top with the egg mix and sprinkle with the chilli flakes, if using.

Bake for 25 minutes or until golden. Let cool for 10 minutes on a cooling rack before serving.

NOTE

These can be served at room temperature or reheated in the oven.

# TOFU KNOT 'CHICKEN WINGS'

TÀU HỦ KI - CÁNH GÀ CHIÊN NƯỚC MẮM CHAY

These are delicious starters or party snacks and are also fantastic on vermicelli noodle salad bowls, complemented by lovely fruit preserves which play on the perfect Vietnamese balance of sweet, sour, umami and heat.

Serves 2
Prep time — 15 minutes
Soaking time — 1 hour
Cooking time — 15–20 minutes

12–15 dried tofu knots, soaked in hot water for 1 hour
4 tablespoons cooking oil

For the batter

60 g (2 oz/½ cup) cornflour (cornstarch)
¼ teaspoon ground turmeric
½ teaspoon ground ginger
¼ teaspoon caster (superfine) sugar
pinch of sea salt

For the buttery apricot sauce

1 tablespoon ghee or butter
1 garlic clove, finely chopped
2 bird's eye chillies, finely chopped
1 tablespoon apricot jam
1 tablespoon fish sauce

For the garnish

zest and juice of ½ lime
toasted sesame seeds
10 g (⅓ oz) coriander (cilantro) leaves, chopped
2 spring onions (scallions), sliced
1 bird's eye chilli, sliced at a diagonal

After soaking, drain the tofu knots in a colander for 10 minutes. Meanwhile, mix the batter ingredients together on a large plate. Then add the still-moist tofu knots onto the plate and evenly coat them in the batter. Get into all the nooks and crannies.

Heat 2 tablespoons of the oil in a frying pan (skillet) over a medium heat, gently place the tofu knots in the pan and fry for about 5 minutes on one side until golden. Turn on the other side, add the remaining oil and continue frying for another 5 minutes. Then drain off on a paper towel. To keep them warm, leave in a 70°C (160°F) fan oven for no longer than an hour.

To make the sauce, add the ghee and garlic to a small saucepan, and cook over a medium heat until slightly golden, then add the chillies, apricot jam and fish sauce. Mix well together and cook until the jam has dissolved and it is bubbling for a couple of minutes.

To serve, place the fried tofu knots onto a plate and pour the apricot sauce all over. Squeeze over the lime juice, sprinkle with sesame seeds, the coriander, spring onion, chillies and lime zest.

NOTES

If you can not get apricot jam, I find that more citrusy jams like marmalade and grapefruit work best. Even lemon curd works well.

If you can not get tofu knots, use medium firm tofu or coat a variety of vegetables, such as sweet potatoes, pumpkin, aubergine (eggplant) or courgettes (zucchini).

# VIETNAMESE DOUGH STICKS

QUẨY

These are eaten fresh from the fryer as a snack or as dippers with breakfast rice porridge or late-night noodle soups. They serve as a lovely sponge to mop up all the broths and juices. For guilty pleasures, they are also great dipped in condensed milk or coated in sugar like a doughnut. They can be snipped with scissors too and dotted around in a salad. I love to enjoy these with a fresh cup of hot homemade Soya Milk (page 183) in the mornings.

Makes 6
Prep time — 30 minutes
Resting time — 2–4 hours at room temperature or refrigerate overnight
Cooking time — 20 minutes

180 ml (6 fl oz/¾ cup) warm water (45°C/113°F)
1 teaspoon caster (superfine) sugar
1 teaspoon fast-action dried yeast
2 teaspoons cooking oil, plus enough to submerge the dough for deep-frying
200 g (7 oz) strong white (bread) flour, plus extra for dusting
1 teaspoon baking powder
1 teaspoon sea salt

Quickly stir the warm water, caster sugar and yeast together in a jug. Leave to activate for 10 minutes at room temperature. It should foam up. Then mix in the 2 teaspoons of cooking oil.

In a free-standing mixer bowl, mix the flour, baking powder and sea salt together, then add the yeast mixture. Scrape down and combine with a spatula. With a dough hook, knead for 5–8 minutes on low. If you don't have a mixer, combine everything with a spatula in a large mixing bowl and knead by hand for about 5 minutes, until you get a smooth dough.

Rest for 2–4 hours depending on the climate or overnight in an airtight, large container in the refrigerator. The dough should rise four-fold and become very sticky. Dust your hands with flour. Knock the dough back and rest your container of dough at room temperature 1 hour before you shape it.

Once the dough is on a well-dusted surface, it tends to creep and flow like a slow-moving lava, so work quickly. Halve the dough on your work surface. Using your hand, pat out two approximately 10 x 25 cm (4 x 10 in) rectangles and cut into 6 strips of 3 cm (1 in) width. Place one strip of dough on top of another. Lay a chopstick or metal skewer lengthways on top of the doubled-up dough strips and press down to squash the two strips together into one complete dough stick. Repeat with the rest of the dough.

Using a thermometer to check, heat the oil to 200°C (400°F/gas 6) in a wok.

When ready to deep-fry, gently pull one dough stick, so it stretches to fit the width of the wok you're using then gently place it into the oil. Deep-fry one dough stick at a time (two if you've had practise); it will puff up and you must turn it continuously with tongs or chopsticks for about 3 minutes until it has stopped inflating and become a lovely deep golden colour.

Drain on paper towels and repeat with the other dough sticks. Serve immediately or within a couple of hours.

NOTE

Any leftovers can be refrigerated over a couple of days. To reheat, toss them around in a frying pan.

# RICE PAPER PIZZA

BÁNH TRÁNG NƯỚNG

This brilliantly inventive and flavoursome snack can have as many or as few ingredients as you like. The textures are incredible, ranging from crispy to crunchy, soft and mellow, hot and fresh. The simplicity of ingredients is what I love best here.

Makes 4
Prep time — 10 minutes
Cooking time — 30 minutes

Equipment
grill rack with legs

8 sheets of 22-cm (8⅔-in) diameter rice paper
120 g (4 oz) asparagus or sugar snap peas, thinly sliced
12 quail's eggs or 2 beaten hen's eggs

For the spring onion oil (page 210)

For the garnish
30 g (1 oz) coriander (cilantro) leaves
30 g (1 oz) Thai basil (optional)
2 tablespoons shop-bought crispy chilli oil (optional)
sriracha (optional)
Kewpie mayo (optional)

To make the spring onion oil, in a medium frying pan, follow the instructions on page 210 and set aside.

On a cutting board, lay a sheet of rice paper and spread ½ tablespoon of spring onion oil evenly over the paper, then lay another sheet of rice paper directly on top. Press the sheets together so that they stick. Scatter the asparagus on top and crack 3 quail's eggs onto them.

Place the grill rack on a gas stove, turn on a low flame, place the rice paper pizza onto it and gently move the sheets around every 10 seconds with tongs or cooking chopsticks to crisp up. Cook until it is crispy everywhere and the egg whites are opaque. I like my yolks runny. If you don't like runny eggs, use beaten eggs instead and drizzle 2 tablespoons over the rice paper pizza and cook until cooked. This should take about 4–5 minutes. Repeat with the other sheets of rice paper.

To serve, sprinkle over the coriander and Thai basil (if using) and a drizzle of crispy chilli oil (if using) and/or sriracha or Kewpie mayo (if using).

If you do not have a gas stove, heat a chargrill pan over a medium-high heat for 5 minutes and place your rice paper onto it, then follow the instructions above without the need to move the paper. You can also do the same in a grill oven for 3–4 minutes.

NOTE

Feel free to create your own toppings, use Crispy Shallots (page 208) and its oil too. Use your deli counter produce and have a refrigerator raid. Snacks don't come better than this.



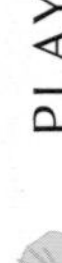

# RICE IS LIFE: AND

TWO

# WHAT TO EAT WITH IT

The British talk about the weather; the Vietnamese talk about rice, saying *'Ăn cỏm chủa?'* (Have you eaten rice yet?).

When my family arrived in Britain as refugees, we had help from charities like the British Red Cross and Save the Children. They introduced us to Mr and Mrs Holland, who were kind and lovely smiley Australians who lived in the UK. On Mondays, after school, they would turn up at 4pm on the dot to help my mother with English lessons and any life things that needed sorting. They primed my younger brother and me with lessons in maths, English and, my favourite of all, geography. I learned about all the places they had travelled to and lived in; all the capital cities in the world from a globe they gifted me. We regarded the Hollands as grandparents, and they even turned up at school plays and parents' evenings.

Every Monday, our regular meals were dialled up a few notches because my mother wanted to show her gratitude, respect and appreciation to Mr and Mrs Holland through the most delicious spreads, all based around rice (so-called 'rice meals'). At the table, they talked about Western dinner manners, how to use a knife and fork, not talking with your mouth full, elbows off the table, saying 'please', not burping and so on... all the opposites of Vietnamese culture where people would generally sit on the floor to eat, sharing meals together and even giving a loud burp at the end of the meal to show their appreciation. It was all very different, but I remember savouring these new 'civilised' manners and ways of being 'proper' for any future occasions.

When my mother found coriander (cilantro) for the first time, she fried a fish and alongside that, she served a fragrant *canh chua* (page 154), a sweet and sour tomato, celery and lime soup with plenty of coriander, plus fried Water Spinach with Capers (page 43), Asparagus Egg Terrine (page 55) and Lemongrass Tofu (page 65) with steamed jasmine rice.

It was 1986. I still remember the day well because Mrs Holland was so mesmerised by the aroma of coriander and the taste she had never experienced before. It was as if she had entered heaven. They rejoiced in the sharing, family-style meal. By eating this way, they got to know bit about our culture and how we ate in Vietnam, by sharing everything. Seeing their happiness and joy made me equally happy. It has always stayed with me. I think it is why I love to cook for people.

It was the saddest day when Mr and Mrs Holland moved back to Australia when we were young teenagers. After they visited us for the last time, we waved goodbye from the fourth floor as always, they blew kisses, waved back and drove off in their golden beige car. Before she passed away at the age of 93, Mrs Holland sent back to me my letters and artwork she had kept after all those years and I read a few excerpts from her diaries about all the lovely rice meals they had together with us.

The following is a selection of dishes to be served with steamed rice to form part of the perfect rice meal.

# EASY GREENS STIR-FRIED WITH GARLIC

RAU TẬP TÀNG XÀO TỎI

Harvest or buy seasonally and celebrate vegetables as great additions to your rice meals. Have everything ready for a blast in the wok.

Makes 4
Prep time — 10 minutes
Cooking time — 30 minutes

Ideas and suggestions

400 g (14 oz) of any or a mix of the following, slice or cut into bite-size lengths

Firmer vegetables

Tenderstem broccoli
cauliflower
broccoli
green beans
runner beans
courgettes (zucchini)
chayotes
okra
baby corn

Leaves – no need to blanch

Chinese broccoli (kai lan) leaves
cime di rapa (broccoli rabe)
pak choi (bok choi)
Chinese mustard leaves
Chinese violets
water spinach
Swiss chard
horseradish leaves
sweet potato leaves
mugwort leaves
sweetheart (hispi) cabbage
kale
cavolo nero

NOTE

If you do not wish to fry the vegetables, you can enjoy them after blanching them with a simple sauce and optional toppings.

Basic ingredients

1 tablespoon rapeseed (canola) or neutral cooking oil or ghee
4 garlic cloves, sliced
1½ tablespoons soy sauce or vegetarian oyster sauce

Optional seasonings: use one of these instead of vegetarian oyster sauce and/or soy sauce

1 teaspoon fermented tofu
1 heaped teaspoon miso plus 1 tablespoon water, mixed
1 tablespoon Homemade Vegan Fish Sauce (page 193)
1 tablespoon Yondu vegetable umami sauce
1 teaspoon mushroom seasoning powder
1 teaspoon Swiss bouillon powder
1 tablespoon nutritional yeast

Optional toppings

1 tablespoon Lemongrass and Chilli Oil (page 210)
1 tablespoon shop-bought crispy or standard chilli oil
1 teaspoon sesame oil
1 teaspoon toasted sesame seeds
as many chilli (hot pepper) flakes as you like
flaked almonds
chopped nuts
nori flakes

Bring 750 ml (25 fl oz/3 cups) water to the boil, blanch the vegetables for a minute then shock in a cold-water bath for 30 seconds before draining. (This keeps the greens looking green.)

In a wok or frying pan (skillet) over a medium-high heat, add the oil and fry the garlic until it starts to turn golden and char at the edges. Add the blanched vegetables with the seasoning and toss for a minute (a couple longer if you have harder vegetables). Serve on a platter as is or add toppings.

# WATER SPINACH WITH CAPERS

RAU MUỐNG XÀO BẠCH HOA

I am always a little anxious when I see my mum cook water spinach (aka morning glory). She stands there, one hip perched against the stove around all the bubbling pots, sizzling pans and raising steam with a small frying pan overfilled with a mountain of morning glory, stems falling here and there! Her chopsticks hover around, sort of poking into it but not really stirring. Is it because she likes cute, little things that she can't use a larger pan? By the time I question all of this, the morning glory has wilted and she's cooking away, shaking out sauces from bottles and suddenly it's on the plate. I've diverted from tradition here and added capers. It pairs marvellously!

Serves 2–4
Prep time — 5 minutes
Cooking time — 5 minutes

½ tablespoon ghee
2 garlic cloves, sliced
200 g (7 oz) water spinach (morning glory), cut into 10 cm (4 in) lengths including stems
½ tablespoon black bean sauce
½ tablespoon vegetarian oyster sauce
½ tablespoon light soy sauce
pinch of chilli (hot pepper) flakes (optional)
1 tablespoon capers, rinsed

In a hot wok over a high heat, add the ghee and garlic. Toss around until the garlic starts to char on its sides then immediately add the water spinach leaves and stems with the black bean sauce, vegetarian oyster sauce, soy sauce and chilli flakes, if using. Quickly stir-fry and toss everything together. This should take about 2 minutes. Then add the capers, quickly mix them in and serve immediately as a side dish with rice.

# BEAN SPROUTS WITH SAMPHIRE

GIÁ XÀO RAU THÌA LÀ BIỂN

Samphire and bean sprouts seem like the perfect match, as both have a similar crunchy texture, one like the sea-salty marshes and one like the earthy land.

Serves 2–4
Prep time — 5 minutes
Cooking time — 3 minutes

½ tablespoon sesame oil
1 garlic clove, sliced
200 g (7 oz) bean sprouts
100 g (3½ oz) samphire
1 tablespoon perilla sauce or Yondu vegetable umami sauce
20 g (¾ oz) garlic chives, snipped into 5 cm (2 in) lengths
½ sheet of nori, snipped into 5 mm (¼ in) strips
1 teaspoon toasted sesame seeds
½ teaspoon crushed pink peppercorns

In a wok or frying pan (skillet) over a high heat, add the sesame oil and garlic. As soon as the garlic starts to turn golden, throw in the bean sprouts, samphire and perilla sauce and quickly stir-fry. Stir in the garlic chives and as soon as everything starts to wilt by half, dish up on a serving platter. Sprinkle with the nori strips, sesame seeds and pink peppercorns.

# SWEET AND SOUR CAULIFLOWER

BÔNG CẢI TRẮNG XÀO CHUA NGỌT

Sweet and sour dishes are rightly popular and a great way to take in plenty of vegetables. With the right balance, they make for a delightful midweek supper or a homemade weekend 'takeaway (takeout)'. Feel free to add sliced carrot and courgettes (zucchini), frozen peas, baby corn and anything you have going into the mix.

Serves 2–4
Prep time — 40 minutes
Cooking time — 30 minutes

For the marinade

1 tablespoon light soy sauce
2 teaspoons caster (superfine) sugar
1 teaspoon sesame oil
½ teaspoon white pepper
1 teaspoon garlic powder
500 g (1 lb 2 oz) cauliflower florets

For the sweet and sour sauce

2 tablespoons white wine or rice vinegar
4 tablespoons brown sugar
100 ml (3½ fl oz/scant ½ cup) vegetable stock (make from half a stock cube)
3 tablespoons ketchup
2 teaspoons tomato purée (paste)
2 tablespoons pineapple juice, from tin used for the vegetables
½ teaspoon cornflour (cornstarch)
1 tablespoon light soy sauce

For the vegetables

2 eggs, beaten in a shallow bowl
100 g (3½ oz/generous ¾ cup) cornflour (cornstarch), plus more for dusting
cooking oil, for deep-frying
1 tablespoon ghee
1 onion, sliced into eighths
2 garlic cloves, finely chopped
½ red (bell) pepper, sliced into 2 cm (¾ in) wide strips
150 g (5 oz) courgette (zucchini), cut into thin long strips
100 g (3½ oz) mangetout (snow peas) or sugar snap peas
100 g (3½ oz) any variety of mushrooms, sliced bite-size
100 g (3½ oz) cherry tomatoes, halved
small tin (about 225 g (8 oz)) of pineapple chunks

For the garnish

2 spring onions (scallions), sliced
20 g (¾ oz) coriander (cilantro) leaves, chopped
20 g (¾ oz) cashews, toasted, coarsely chopped
a few slices of red chilli (optional)
sprinkle of toasted sesame seeds (optional)
zest and juice of ½ lime

In a large bowl, mix all the marinade ingredients together and set aside.

Mix together all the ingredients for the sweet and sour sauce. Set aside.

Have three shallow bowls ready – one for the beaten egg, one for cornflour and one to place the coated cauliflower. Dip a cauliflower floret in the beaten egg, then dredge it with cornflour and tap off any excess flour, then place it in the third bowl and repeat with all the florets.

In a wok or deep frying pan (skillet), add about 2.5 cm (1 in) depth of cooking oil and bring to about 170°C (325°F). Deep-fry the coated cauliflower for exactly 4 minutes until they turn golden then set to cool on a rack or paper towels. For a crispier affair, recoat the cauliflower in cornflour and double fry, the second time for 2 minutes at 170°C (325°F).

In the same wok, over a high heat, add the ghee. Once it has melted, add the onions to char on the edges and then the garlic. Once the garlic starts to turn golden, throw in the red pepper, courgette and mangetout. Quickly stir-fry and toss for about 2 minutes then add the mushrooms. Continue to fry for 3 more minutes then add the cherry tomatoes and pineapple chunks. Mix together then add the sweet and sour sauce. Toss and cook together until it becomes juicy, thick, saucy and glossy. Turn off the heat and fold in the cauliflower florets.

Garnish with the spring onion, coriander, cashews, chilli and sesame seeds, if using, and a squeeze of lime and a sprinkle of zest. Serve immediately with steamed rice.

# GRILLED AUBERGINES WITH SPRING ONION OIL

CÀ TÍM NƯỚNG MỠ HÀNH

This very quick and easy recipe uses just a few humble and simple ingredients. It is a delightful summery dish, which is ever so inviting. Don't be afraid to char and blacken the aubergines (eggplants), as this contributes to a deep, smoky complexity to the creamy, soft flesh.

Serves 2
Prep time — 10 minutes
Cooking time — 25 minutes

2 long aubergines (eggplants) or graffiti aubergines
2 tablespoons neutral cooking oil
2 spring onions (scallions), sliced
pinch of sea salt

For the dressing

zest and juice of ½ lime
2 tablespoons sugar
2 tablespoons Yondu vegetable umami sauce, soy sauce or Homemade Vegan Fish Sauce (page 193)
1 bird's eye chilli, sliced thinly at a diagonal (optional)
1 teaspoon toasted sesame seeds

For the garnish

1 tablespoon roasted, salted peanuts, roughly chopped (optional)

Place a griddle pan on the stove and heat it up until hot. Prick the aubergines with a fork or skewer and place them, whole, on the pan to char for about 15–20 minutes, turning every 5 minutes.

Meanwhile, add the oil to a small saucepan over a low heat with the spring onions and salt. Simmer until the spring onions start to soften and immediately remove from the heat.

Mix the dressing ingredients together in a small bowl.

Once the aubergines are cooked, let them cool slightly, then peel off and discard the skin. If using fatter aubergines, use a knife or your hands to peel the flesh of the aubergines lengthways into 4 parts and lay on a serving plate. Slice them into bite-size pieces. Pour the dressing over the aubergines and sprinkle with the peanuts, if using. Serve with steamed jasmine rice, alongside other dishes including pickles. Or use as a topping on vermicelli noodle salad bowls (page 137).

NOTE

If you don't have a griddle pan, you can cook this over a grill rack or in a fan oven at 200°C (400°F/gas 6). Place two aubergines on a baking tray (pan) and bake for 30 minutes. You can also cook this on the barbecue.

# BLACK BEAN AUBERGINES

CÀ TÍM XÀO SỐT TƯƠNG ĐEN

The enticing, seared golden criss-cross on these aubergine (eggplant) slices is definitely a crowd-pleaser. Don't tell anyone how easy this is to prepare. Note that shop-bought black bean sauces will vary from brand to brand; some may be sweeter and others may be saltier. Adjust accordingly, add sugar or maple syrup if needed or, if salty, use less and mellow out with a splash of water and reduce the soy sauce. Always taste and balance out the flavours.

Serves 4
Prep time — 10 minutes
Cooking time — 20 minutes

2 aubergines (eggplants)
2 tablespoons rapeseed (canola) oil
2 teaspoons ghee
4 garlic cloves, crushed or finely chopped
20 g (¾ oz) spring onions (scallions), sliced thinly lengthways
3–4 tablespoons black bean sauce
1 tablespoon soy sauce
1 teaspoon maple syrup
squeeze of lemon or lime juice, plus zest
1 bird's eye chilli, sliced (optional)

Slice the aubergine lengthways into 4 x 1 cm (½ in) thick pieces. Using a sharp knife, score lines 3 mm (¼ in) into the flesh to make a grid on both sides. Using a pastry brush, thinly paint the oil on all sides of the aubergine.

In a large frying pan (skillet) over a high heat, place the slices of aubergine flat onto the pan and sear for 5 minutes on each side. Set aside in a single layer on a serving platter.

In a small saucepan over a medium heat, add the ghee and cook the garlic until it catches colour, then add the spring onions, black bean sauce, soy sauce and maple syrup. Bring to a simmer for 2–3 minutes then pour all over the surface of the seared aubergine slices. To serve, squeeze over lime juice plus its zest and bird's eye chilli (if using).

Serve as a side dish or enjoy with steamed rice, sticky rice with mung beans or vermicelli noodle salad bowls (page 137).

## NOTES

Make the sauce ahead of time without the spring onions (scallions), and when ready to serve, reheat with spring onions. You can also sear the aubergines (eggplants) ahead and keep warm in a 70°C (158°F) fan oven or reheat in the microwave when ready to serve. Feel free to use extra herbs like coriander (cilantro) leaves and Thai basil, garnish with fresh chilli or flakes, toasted sesame seeds, nori strips, nuts and seeds.

# EGG AND TOMATO SCRAMBLE

TRỨNG XÀO CÀ CHUA

The simplest of ingredients make some of the most enjoyable meals. I love having a jar of fermented tofu around which gives a nice oomph to this dish.

Serves 2
Prep time — 5 minutes
Cooking time — 5 minutes

1 tablespoon rapeseed (canola) oil
2 small round shallots, sliced
2 garlic cloves, roughly chopped
10 g (⅓ oz) fresh ginger root, finely chopped
200 g (7 oz) cherry tomatoes, halved
(or any other tomatoes, diced)
2 teaspoons fermented tofu, mashed
50 ml (1¾ fl oz) coconut water or water
1 tablespoon vegetarian oyster sauce
4 eggs, beaten
1 spring onion (scallion), sliced
20 g (¾ oz) coriander (cilantro) leaves

In a hot wok or frying pan (skillet) over a medium-high heat, add the oil, shallots, garlic and ginger and fry until golden and fragrant. Throw in the cherry tomatoes, let them sizzle for a minute, then add the fermented tofu, coconut water and vegetarian oyster sauce. Stir, toss and fry until the tomatoes have collapsed a little. Add the eggs and spring onion. Swirl the pan to get it covering all the sides and sprinkle over the coriander.

Working quickly before the egg sets, use a pair of cooking chopsticks to drag the cooked egg to the centre from the edges. Let the uncooked egg mixture pool into the gaps left behind, cover and cook for a minute or until the egg is completely cooked.

Serve immediately with steamed rice or on toasted bread.

# ASPARAGUS EGG TERRINE

TRỨNG CHƯNG



This is traditionally served with broken rice (*cơm tấm*), pickles, stir-fried greens and a vegetable soup. In hard times, people tend to make this very salty so that it can stretch a long way with lots of perfectly steamed rice. Fillings can vary and dried or fresh mushrooms are a great addition. It is also great as a sliced topping for noodle soups or served cold in *bánh mì* and summer rolls.

Serves 3–4
Prep time — 15 minutes
Cooking time — 25 minutes

½ tablespoon ghee
1 shallot, sliced
2 garlic cloves, finely chopped
40 g (1½ oz) leek, finely sliced
½ tablespoon cooking oil
20–25 g (¾ oz) glass noodles, soaked 10 minutes, snipped into 5 cm (2 in) lengths
90–100 g (3½ oz) asparagus, woody ends removed, sliced into 3 cm (1 in) pieces
4 eggs, beaten
½ teaspoon mushroom seasoning powder
1 teaspoon fermented tofu, mashed or 2 tablespoons Worcestershire sauce
pinch of freshly ground black pepper
2 teaspoons light soy sauce
2 egg yolks

In a small frying pan (skillet) over a medium heat, add the ghee, shallot, garlic and leek, and fry for about 4 minutes until golden.

Use the oil to grease a large, steam-proof porcelain or glass bowl. Then add the noodles, asparagus, eggs (but not the two separate yolks), mushroom seasoning powder, fermented tofu, pepper and soy sauce.

If not using a bamboo steamer, wrap a clean tea towel (dish towel) around the lid of a steamer or saucepan, stand the bowl on a steamer basket inside the steamer with a 2.5 cm (1 in) depth of boiling water and steam for 20 minutes, checking levels occasionally and top up the water if necessary. Then beat the yolks and pour over the top, before steaming for another 5 minutes.

# MIXED VEGETABLE CURRY

CÀ RI CHAY

The ingredients list looks long, but I like to pack it with plenty of vegetables. Put it all into a casserole dish (Dutch oven) or large saucepan. Great for a midweek supper. Enjoy any leftovers on toast.

Serves 2
Prep time — 15–20 minutes
Cooking time — 15 minutes

1 tablespoon rapeseed (canola) oil
2 shallots, sliced
3 garlic cloves, sliced
15 g (½ oz) fresh turmeric, peeled, finely chopped (or 1 teaspoon ground turmeric)
15 g (½ oz) fresh ginger root, finely chopped
2 lemongrass stalks, bashed, cut into 5 cm (2 in) lengths
120 g (4 oz) cherry tomatoes, whole
200 g (7 oz) cauliflower, broken into bite-size florets
110 g (3⅔ oz) king oyster mushrooms, cut into 2 cm (¾ in) rounds
50 g (1¾ oz) fine green beans, cut into 4 cm (1½ in) lengths
50 g (1¾ oz) baby courgettes (zucchini), cut into 2 cm (¾ in) rounds
50 g (1¾ oz) carrots, cut into 2 cm (¾ in) cubes
100 g (3½ oz) potatoes, cut into 2 cm (¾ in) cubes
2 large mild red chillies
1 teaspoon chilli powder (optional)
1 teaspoon curry powder
200 ml (7 fl oz/scant 1 cup) coconut milk
½ teaspoon mushroom seasoning powder or 1 tablespoon nutritional yeast
½ teaspoon sea salt
½ teaspoon sugar
100 ml (3½ fl oz/scant ½ cup) water or coconut water
20 g (¾ oz) Thai basil leaves
20 g (¾ oz) coriander (cilantro) leaves
juice of ½ lime

In a deep frying pan (skillet) or a casserole dish (Dutch oven) with a lid, add the oil, shallots and garlic over a medium heat. Let them take some colour then add the turmeric, ginger and lemongrass. Let this fry for a few minutes until fragrant and then add all the vegetables, including the chillies and chilli powder (if using). Evenly sprinkle the curry powder all over. Let everything sit for 3 minutes or so and then stir to coat the vegetables with the curry powder.

Pour over the coconut milk, season with the mushroom seasoning powder, sea salt, sugar and splash over the water to further steam the vegetables. Mix well. Put a lid on and cook for 10 minutes.

To serve, remove the lemongrass and garnish with the Thai basil, coriander and lime juice. This is excellent with steamed jasmine rice or sticky rice with mung beans.

# SWEET AND SOUR VEGETABLE STIR-FRY

RAU XÀO CHUA NGỌT

For me, these are the flavours of homecoming, to Phan Thiết, my mother's hometown. My cousins, Thúy and Thảo, take care of my culinary adventures with great zeal and dedication. Sometimes we would go 'food shopping' together where Thảo would buy one celery stalk, exactly four tomatoes and a few sprigs of herbs, just enough of what is needed for this dish and no more. This ensures that all their cooking is at its best, with the freshest of ingredients and nothing going to waste. For extra texture and protein, add Salt and Pepper Tofu (page 62) or tofu puff.

Serves 4 as sharing dish
Prep time — 15 minutes
Cooking time — 7 minutes

4 garlic cloves
2 teaspoons coconut sugar or brown sugar
1 bird's eye chilli, roughly cut
1 tablespoon cooking oil or ghee
1 red onion, sliced into 1 cm (½ in) strips
1 celery stalk, sliced into 6 cm (2⅓ in) strips at a diagonal
4 tomatoes, cut into eighths
½ courgette (zucchini), cut at a diagonal into 5 mm (¼ in) slices
10 cm (4 in) cucumber, sliced into 3 cm (1 in) chunks
200 g (7 oz) fresh or tinned pineapple
100 ml (3½ fl oz/scant ½ cup) pineapple or orange juice (or juice from the tin)
1 tablespoon capers, rinsed
1 teaspoon cornflour (cornstarch) mixed with 100 ml (3½ fl oz/scant ½ cup) water
3 tablespoons perilla sauce or Homemade Vegan Fish Sauce (page 193)
zest and juice of ½ lime or lemon
fresh herbs of choice, to garnish

Pound the garlic, coconut sugar and chilli into a paste with a pestle and mortar and set to one side.

Heat the cooking oil over a high heat in a wok or frying pan (skillet). When it is very hot, add the onion. Let it sit for a minute to char the edges then add the celery, tomatoes and the pounded paste.

Stir-fry vigorously for a minute then add the courgette, cucumber, pineapple, fruit juice, capers, cornflour mixture and perilla sauce. Stir, toss and fry for 3 minutes then squeeze over the lime or lemon juice, adding the zest.

Serve immediately with a garnish of any fresh herbs on steamed rice or crispy noodles (page 200).

# TOFU

ĐẬU HỦ TRẮNG

Tofu, also known as bean curd, is made from curdling soya-bean milk. Some tofu is soft, like silken tofu which has a higher water content, whereas extra-firm tofu is at the other side of the spectrum. I really love silken tofu. It is slightly harder to handle, but I don't mind if it becomes mashed up within a dish. The taste and fragrance really come across in good quality silken tofu. If I'm not using silken tofu, I use medium-firm tofu because it still has a soft texture but holds its structure. I do not generally use firm (cotton) or extra-firm tofu.

Tofu is much loved in Vietnamese cuisine and it will often make an appearance at the dinner table because it is delicious and is considered a rightful ingredient in itself and not a meat substitute.

Shop-bought tofu puffs are brilliant toppings, great in noodle soups where they hold broth like a sponge, and bean-curd skins can be used to make Vegan Vietnamese Sausages (page 117) and add a source of protein to braised dishes.

For the golden-fried tofu

**2 tablespoons vegetable oil**
**1 pinch of Maldon salt**
**400 g (14 oz) medium-firm tofu, patted dry, sliced into desired shape**

Heat a large frying pan (skillet) over a medium heat, add half the oil and sprinkle the salt over the surface of the pan, then fry the tofu for about 8 minutes on each side until golden. Remove from the heat and drain the tofu on paper towels.

From here on, add to different stir fries and soups. Make a balanced dressing to dip in or fry with tomatoes (see Tofu and Tomatoes with Spinach and Basil, page 70).



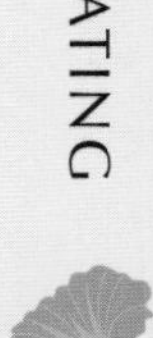

# SALT AND PEPPER TOFU

ĐẬU HỦ XỐC MUỐI TIÊU

This is a great topping to enhance stir-fries, noodle soups or a crispy vessel to carry delicious sauces.

Serves 2–4
Prep time — 10 minutes
Cooking time — 10 minutes

300 g (10½ oz) medium-firm tofu
70 g (2½ oz/generous ½ cup) potato starch or cornflour (cornstarch)
¼ teaspoon ground ginger
¼ teaspoon cayenne pepper
¼ teaspoon sea salt
½ teaspoon caster (superfine) sugar
½ teaspoon baking powder
½ teaspoon freshly ground black pepper
3 tablespoons cooking oil

Remove the tofu from its packaging and pat dry. Cut into desired shapes such as batons, squares or cubes.

In a large plate or shallow bowl, mix the potato starch, ground ginger, cayenne pepper, sea salt, caster sugar, baking powder and black pepper. Add the tofu and gently toss around so that every piece is covered in the flour mix.

In a wok or frying pan (skillet), heat the oil over a medium heat and fry the tofu pieces until each side is golden and crispy. Alternatively, deep-fry at 160°C (320°F) until golden. Serve with noodles, rice, vegetables or with a dipping sauce of choice (page 212). Feel free to drizzle over spring onion oil (page 210) or crispy shallots (page 208).

# LEMONGRASS TOFU

ĐẬU HŨ KHO SẢ

I like using medium-firm tofu, but understanding the correct firmness of tofu will really help make your veggie dishes amazing, as tofu takes on all the fabulous flavours you throw at it. As well as being a great topping for a noodle salad bowl, this is a much-loved dish to be shared with friends and family during a meal of rice and lots of other dishes. This is also great for summer rolls or *bánh mì* filling, therefore a must-have in your repertoire.

Serves 2–4
Prep time — 15 minutes
Cooking time — 25 minutes

1 shallot, finely chopped
2 garlic cloves, finely chopped
1 (or 2) bird's eye chilli, finely chopped (optional)
1 lemongrass stalk, finely chopped
1 tablespoon premium quality soy sauce or Homemade Vegan Fish Sauce (page 193)
1½ tablespoons vegetarian oyster sauce
1½ tablespoons maple syrup
1 tablespoon black vinegar (or cider vinegar)
300 g (10½ oz) medium-firm tofu, sliced into 1 cm (½ in) batons
2 tablespoons cooking oil
50 ml (1¾ fl oz) coconut water or aloe vera juice
30 g (1 oz) coriander (cilantro) leaves or Thai basil, coarsely chopped
1 tablespoon toasted sesame seeds

NOTE

If you would like to deep-fry the tofu, fry the other ingredients in another frying pan, then combine the sauce with the tofu when the tofu is golden and crispy.

Mix the shallot, garlic, chilli and lemongrass in a large bowl, together with the soy sauce, vegetarian oyster sauce, maple syrup and vinegar. Add the sliced tofu to the bowl and marinate for at least 30 minutes or in the refrigerator overnight.

In a large frying pan (skillet) over a medium heat, add the oil, then place the tofu batons clockwise to fry 5 minutes on each side or until golden. Then add the rest of the marinade and the coconut water to sizzle for a further 3–5 minutes, adding more if too dry. Stir in the coriander at the last minute.

Sprinkle with the sesame seeds and serve immediately with steamed rice or on vermicelli noodle salad bowls (page 137).

# SPICED TOFU WITH AUBERGINE AND ENOKI MUSHROOMS

CÀ TÍM SỐT CAY TỨ XUYÊN

You can do all sorts of amazing things with aubergines (eggplants); I love aubergines! They soak up any sort of magic you throw at them. I often buy a jar of ready-made spicy bean paste when I stock up on my storecupboard supplies. It quickly helps me achieve the special, spicy umami flavours with the smoky luxurious aubergines and coat the silken tofu cubes in a lava of chilli oil. This sublime dish makes its appearance at my dinner table on a regular rotation.

Serves 4
Prep time — 10 minutes
Cooking time — 45 minutes

2 aubergines (eggplants)
2 tablespoons rapeseed (canola) oil
3 shallots, sliced
25 g (¾ oz) fresh ginger root, finely chopped
4 garlic cloves, roughly chopped
1 teaspoon Sichuan peppercorns, grinded (optional)
100 g (3½ oz) enoki mushrooms, halved lengthways if too fat
½ red (bell) pepper, diced into 5 mm (¼ in) cubes
1 tablespoon vegetarian oyster sauce
2 tablespoons spicy bean sauce
2 tablespoons soy sauce or Homemade Vegan Fish Sauce (page 193)
1 tablespoon tomato purée (paste)
1 teaspoon fermented tofu, mashed
100 ml (3½ fl oz) coconut water
300 g (10½ oz) silken tofu, cut into cubes
20 g (¾ oz) coriander (cilantro) or Thai basil, roughly chopped
1 teaspoon pink pepper (or black pepper), crushed
2 tablespoons crispy chilli oil (Laoganman)
Lemongrass and Chilli Oil (page 210)

Place the aubergines over the flame of two gas hobs, which are set to a medium heat. Turn the aubergines every couple of minutes and cook until all areas are soft and almost falling apart (about 6–8 minutes). If you don't have a gas hob, you can cook the aubergines in a fan oven at 200°C (400°F/gas 6) for 25 minutes.

Once the aubergines are cooked, scoop the flesh out into a bowl, and discard the skin. Set aside.

In a medium-hot wok or frying pan (skillet), add the oil, shallot, ginger and garlic and fry for a couple of minutes. Mix in the Sichuan peppercorns (if using) then throw in the mushrooms and red pepper, stir-fry for a moment then add the vegetarian oyster sauce, spicy bean sauce, soy sauce, tomato purée and mashed fermented tofu. Stir-fry for 2 minutes to mix in all the flavours. The pan will be dry at this point, so add the coconut water to loosen and cook for another 2 minutes. Add the silken tofu cubes and gently fold into the aubergine and mushroom mix. Gently fold in the coriander or Thai basil, being careful not to break too many tofu cubes. Let it sizzle for another couple of minutes.

To serve, season with crushed pepper and crispy chilli oil or homemade lemongrass and chilli oil.



NOTE

Use any kind of mushrooms you desire.

# STUFFED TOMATOES WITH TOFU, MUSHROOMS AND CAPERS

CÀ CHUA DỒN ĐẬU HỦ

This is a typical and favourite dish to bring to the table with an array of other plates to share with rice. Buy firm, same-size, round tomatoes; overripe tomatoes will turn to mush. For ease, this recipe uses an oven, but it can be sautéed in a large frying pan (skillet) with a lid to steam.

Serves 4
Prep time — 10 minutes
Cooking time — 35 minutes

1 tablespoon cooking oil
4 garlic cloves, finely chopped
160 g (5⅔ oz) oyster mushrooms, thinly sliced
200 g (7 oz) silken tofu, crumbled
2½ tablespoons soy sauce
2 tablespoons maple syrup
2 tablespoons ponzu or cider vinegar
2 spring onions (scallions), sliced
1 tablespoon capers, rinsed
4 firm tomatoes, heritage, beef or ordinary
1 tablespoon rapeseed (canola) or other neutral oil
2 tablespoons panko breadcrumbs
sea salt and freshly ground black pepper

For the sauce

1 teaspoon cooking oil
2 garlic cloves, finely chopped
2 teaspoons soy sauce or Homemade Vegan Fish Sauce (page 193)
pinch of sugar
2 teaspoons cornflour (cornstarch), mixed with 1 tablespoon water to form a slurry
2 teaspoons lime juice
1 tablespoon coriander (cilantro) stalks, roughly chopped

For the garnish

spring onion (scallion), coriander (cilantro), mint or Thai basil

Preheat a fan oven to 200°C (400°F/gas 6).

Heat a wok or frying pan (skillet), over a medium-high heat, add the cooking oil and fry the garlic until golden. Add the mushrooms, stirring to combine and fry for 2 minutes, then add the tofu, soy sauce, maple syrup and ponzu. Stir-fry, breaking the tofu into 1 cm (½ in) pieces and then add the spring onion and capers. Continue frying for a minute, turn off the heat and set aside.

Slice off the top quarter of each tomato and scoop out the pulp. Dice the tops and pulp and set aside. Then pack the hollow tomatoes as tightly as possible with the mushroom and tofu stuffing. Brush the tomatoes all over with the oil, and sprinkle the breadcrumbs and salt and pepper on top. Place on a baking tray (pan) or smallish casserole dish (Dutch oven). Bake for 25–30 minutes.

For the sauce, add the oil to the same wok and fry the garlic until golden. Add the diced tomato tops and pulp, soy sauce, sugar and cornflour slurry. Cook for 5–7 minutes to form a sauce then add the lime juice and coriander stalks.

Serve the tomatoes with the sauce around it and a garnish of herbs or spring onion.

# TOFU AND TOMATOES WITH SPINACH AND BASIL

ĐẬU HỦ XÀO CÀ CHUA

Sizzling, juicy tomatoes with tofu is a really popular dish at the Vietnamese table; it has a wonderful umami flavour and is quick and easy to prepare. You can actually use any savoury condiment from soy sauce to (vegan) fish sauce. Use any sweet and sour seasoning too, depending on what you have around, for extra goodness. I like to stir in spinach or kale from time to time.

Serves 4 as a sharing dish
Prep time — 5 minutes
Cooking time — 25 minutes

For the tofu

2 tablespoons vegetable oil
pinch of sea salt
400 g (14 oz) medium-firm tofu, cut into 4 cm (1½ in) squares, 1 cm (½ in) thickness

For the vegetables

2 tablespoons cider vinegar
1 tablespoon vegetarian oyster sauce
1 tablespoon soy sauce or vegetable umami seasoning
1 tablespoon maple syrup
1 round shallot, finely chopped
1 garlic clove, finely chopped
350 g (12 oz) tomatoes, any variety, roughly chopped, bite-size
3 spring onions (scallions), sliced diagonally
handful of spinach
3 Thai basil sprigs

Heat a large frying pan (skillet) over a medium heat, add half the oil and the salt and spread over the surface of the pan, then fry the tofu for about 8 minutes on each side until golden. Remove from the heat and drain the tofu on paper towels.

In a small bowl, mix together the cider vinegar, vegetarian oyster sauce, soy sauce and maple syrup as seasoning.

Put the pan back over a medium-high heat, add the remaining oil and brown the shallot, then add the garlic and fry until golden. Add the tomatoes and keep them still for a couple of minutes to brown. Add the fried tofu, then gently turn and stir-fry for a couple of minutes before pouring over the seasoning. Add the spring onions and spinach. Gently stir for another 2 minutes until the spinach wilts.

Garnish with the Thai basil and serve with steamed rice.

# THREE

# SALAD DAYS

# SALAD DAYS



Salads are usually the star of the show in Vietnam, served with crackers or enjoyed with rice and other dishes. Their beautiful and seasonal elements, like mouth-watering green papaya and mango, pink and plump pomelo, pale and sweet pomegranate seeds are considered valuable and precious, reserved for special occasions.

I didn't really know how to cook until my early twenties. My mum made sure that I was nourished as I was growing up, but prioritised my homework over letting me loose in the kitchen, although I was often part of the spring-roll production line and pleated bao buns to perfection and plucked herbs like the wind.

When I grew up, I travelled far from home and found myself craving my mother's cooking, pining for papaya salad and phở. On visits to bare Asian stores with little but vacuum-packed biscuits, instant noodles and jars of what-nots, I tried to recreate the food that I missed. That was how my cooking adventures began.

I came up with versions of Vietnamese salads like strawberry, watermelon and lamb's lettuce dressed with soy, balsamic vinegar and lemon. I used whatever was available: unripe Galia melons, crunchy nectarines and carrot tossed with sugar snap peas, chillies, honey, soy sauce and so on.

I shared these feasts with friends, and the complex flavours and fun and exciting textures thrilled us all, as we sang lustily into the night to the music of everyone from Radiohead to Frank Sinatra. Without knowing it then, those precious salad days steered the direction of my life. I would travel to lose myself only to find myself once more in foreign supermarket aisles, eyeing up bottles and jars, so I could reconstruct my mother's edible palette of many colours.

# MANGO AND MELON SALAD WITH POMELO

XOÀI DƯA LƯỚI BƯỞI SỐT CHANH DÂY

Before the Italians changed their currency to euros, I had a wallet stuffed with hefty lira notes and it was all for a small greengrocer at the bottom of a small, gorgeous mountain village somewhere by the sea shore in Liguria, northern Italy. Its walls were unplastered, the green glass door would hit a chime and one bare light-bulb hung from its ceiling over a beautiful display of the sweetest, furry summer peaches, shapely nectarines, urrowed lemons, plump, crimson cherries and an array of yellow, pale and green courgettes (zucchini), some flowering, wonky and spiky. The perfume of its freshest fruit picked only the day before was exquisite. Choose your melon and mango by their aroma: the stronger the smell, the sweeter the fruit. Balance this sweetness in the dressing that you make; use less honey if the fruits are sweet but more if they are sour.

Serves 4
Prep time — 20 minutes
Cooking time — 20 minutes

For the passion fruit, lemon and honey dressing

½ tablespoon soy sauce or Yondu vegetable umami sauce
pulp and juice of 1 passion fruit
½ tablespoon honey
1 bird's eye chilli, finely sliced
juice of ½ lemon or lime, reserve the zest

For the salad

1 courgette (zucchini), thinly sliced lengthways
½ melon, peeled and sliced into half-moons
1 unripe mango, sliced into thin half-moons
zest of ½ lemon or lime
2 mint sprigs, de-stalked and sliced
⅓ pink pomelo or seeds of ⅓ pomegranate

Mix all the dressing ingredients in a small bowl.

Place the courgette slices in a hot griddle pan turning once until there are satisfying char marks on both sides. Set aside to cool.

Scatter the melon, mango and courgette on a platter. Toss together. Drizzle the dressing all over the top and garnish with the lemon zest, mint and pink pomelo or pomegranate seeds.

NOTE

If you cannot get hold of pink pomelo, use pink grapefruit or grapefruit. This salad also works well with apple, pear and nectarine slices.

# WATERMELON AND STRAWBERRY SALAD WITH CHILLI SALT

DƯA HẤU, DÂU TÂY TRỘN MUỐI ỚT

Watermelon is commonly served with chilli salt in Vietnam to bring out its unique taste and sweetness.

Serves 4
Prep time — 20 minutes

For the salad dressing

1 tablespoon Yondu vegetable umami sauce
1 tablespoon lime juice
½ tablespoon maple syrup or honey

For the chilli salt

2 teaspoons sea salt flakes
1 bird's eye chilli, finely chopped

For the salad

watercress or lamb's lettuce
2 tablespoons black olives, roughly chopped
500–800 g (1 lb 2 oz–1 lb 12 oz) watermelon, sliced into bite-size cubes, seeds removed
4 strawberries, sliced

Shake the salad dressing ingredients in a jar.

To make the chilli salt, add the salt and chillies to a pestle and mortar and crush together until the salt turns pink.

Arrange the watercress and olives in a salad bowl or platter. Drizzle the dressing over them, then place the watermelon cubes and strawberry slices on top. Serve with the chilli salt to sprinkle or dip the watermelon pieces in.

# GREEN PAPAYA SALAD WITH POMELO, APPLE AND ARTICHOKE

GỎI ĐU ĐỦ TRỘN BƯỞI, TÁO VÀ ATISÔ

Papaya salad showcases the essence of deep and complex Vietnamese flavours. Our salad dressings must be the right balance of sweet, sour, savoury and hot. Good quality sauces play a huge part. As it is not always possible to get hold of these beautiful Asian fruits, crunchy vegetables like carrot and cabbage can help to bulk up salads. How you cut or grate the vegetables has an impact on its overall structure, taste and texture, so it's worth investing in a Vietnamese julienne grater to produce the perfect pieces. Grate lengthways to create long noodle-like strands. Use a peeler to slice thinly, then cut to the perfect shape: too big and it's overwhelming, too small and not satisfying. Never use a blender to julienne vegetables or your salads will be wet and soggy.

Serves 4
Prep time — 30 minutes

For the salad

1 green papaya, peeled and julienned
1 carrot, julienned
100 g (3½ oz) sugar snap peas, veins removed
½ kohlrabi, julienned
1 Pink Lady apple (or any red variety) scored, sliced 3-mm (⅛-in) thick and submerged in water with the juice of ½ lemon, then drained
10 Vietnamese coriander sprigs, leaves only, snipped into 2 cm (¾ in) pieces
300 g (10½ oz) marinaded deli artichokes, drained
¼ pink pomelo, peeled, skin removed and flesh cut into 3 cm (1 in) chunks (optional)
seeds of ½ pomegranate
zest of 1 lime
20 g (¾ oz) coriander (cilantro) sprigs

For the dressing

2 tablespoons maple syrup
3 tablespoons Homemade Vegan Fish Sauce (page 193) or Yondu vegetable umami sauce
3 tablespoons lime juice
2 garlic cloves, crushed
1 bird's eye chilli, finely chopped
3 tablespoons shelled pistachios or salted, roasted peanuts, coarsely chopped or crushed

To serve

shop-bought rice crackers

Mix the papaya, carrot, sugar snap peas, kohlrabi, apple and Vietnamese coriander in a large mixing bowl. Add the artichoke and toss well together.

Mix all the dressing ingredients and pour over the salad. Mix together.

Place onto a serving plate and scatter the pomelo (if using), pomegranate, lime zest and coriander over the salad. Serve immediately with crackers.

# ORANGE, GRILLED PEACH AND TOMATO SALAD

XÀ LÁCH CÀ CHUA, ĐÀO NƯỚNG VÀ CAM

The joys of summer are on this plate, shared with a fresh crusty baguette and cold sparkling water.

Serves 4
Prep time — 20 minutes
Cooking time — 20 minutes

4 peaches, stoned (pitted), quartered
4 small round shallots, sliced
1 tablespoon cider vinegar
1 tablespoon caster (superfine) sugar
¼ teaspoon freshly ground black pepper
4 heritage tomatoes or various summer tomatoes
2 blood oranges or summer oranges

For the marmalade and mustard dressing

1 green bird's eye chilli
1 teaspoon fermented tofu
1 tablespoon perilla sauce, soy sauce, Yondu umami sauce or Homemade Vegan Fish Sauce (page 193)
1 teaspoon English mustard
1 teaspoon marmalade

For the garnish

Thai basil, Vietnamese coriander or mint, sliced, small leaves left whole

In a hot griddle pan, char the peaches on all sides. Set aside to cool.

In a small bowl, mix the shallot with the vinegar, sugar and black pepper and leave to lightly pickle for 15 minutes.

Meanwhile, slice the tomatoes horizontally into thin rounds and place them onto a big platter. Then slice the oranges horizontally into thin rounds, removing the rind and place them on top of the tomatoes. Add the grilled peaches, scatter the pickled shallot over the salad, including any juices.

In a small bowl, mix all the dressing ingredients together.

To serve, drizzle the dressing over the fruit and sprinkle with Thai basil, Vietnamese coriander or mint. Enjoy with baguette slices or crusty bread.

# STUFFED COURGETTE-FLOWER SALAD WITH AUBERGINE, PEAS AND TOFU

BÔNG BÍ NHỒI ĐẬU HỦ VÀ CÀ TÍM

Enjoy with a crusty baguette or with sheets of vermicelli rice noodles. These are a feast for all the senses.

Serves 4
Prep time — 40 minutes
Cooking time — 45 minutes–1 hour

For the salad

2 courgettes (zucchini), sliced lengthways into 5 mm (¼ in) slices
1 graffiti aubergine, sliced lengthways into 5 mm (¼ in) slices
100 g (3½ oz) Tenderstem broccoli, broken into florets
100 g (3½ oz) asparagus, woody end snipped off

For the mango and mint dressing

1 bird's eye chilli, finely chopped
1 garlic clove, crushed
2 tablespoons mango chutney
2 tablespoons Yondu vegetable umami sauce
zest and juice of ½ lime or lemon
10 g (⅓ oz) mint leaves, finely chopped

For the stuffed courgette flowers

1 tablespoon rapeseed (canola) oil
2 garlic cloves, finely chopped
250 g (9 oz) graffiti aubergine, sliced into 5 mm (¼ in) cubes
¼ teaspoon caster (superfine) sugar
¼ teaspoon freshly ground black pepper
2 tablespoons Yondu vegetable umami sauce, umami paste, or vegetable stock paste
100 g (3½ oz) garden peas
150 g (5 oz) silken tofu, coarsely mashed
10 g (⅓ oz) coriander (cilantro) stalks, finely sliced
12 (60 g (2 oz)) courgette flowers, pistil and stamens removed
2 eggs, beaten
4 tablespoons panko breadcrumbs or homemade breadcrumbs
3 tablespoons vegetable oil

NOTE

If courgette (zucchini) flowers are not in season, cook the filling and scatter over the grilled vegetables.

In a hot griddle pan or barbecue, grill the courgette and aubergine slices, broccoli and asparagus until there are char marks. Arrange on a serving platter and set aside.

Mix all the dressing ingredients together in a bowl.

To make the stuffed courgette flowers, add the oil and garlic to a saucepan over a medium heat. When the garlic is brown on the edges, add the aubergine cubes, sugar, pepper and vegetable umami sauce. Cook with the lid on for about 5 minutes to soften the aubergines slightly. Add the peas and mix in the tofu. Cook for 2 minutes, then turn off the heat and let the filling cool to room temperature before gently mixing in the coriander stalks.

Gently stuff each courgette flower tightly with the filling and twist the ends of the petals together to hold in place.

On a plate, add the beaten egg and on another plate, add the breadcrumbs. Dip each stuffed flower in the egg, coating all the nooks and crannies, then roll each one on the breadcrumb plate to coat in crumbs.

Heat the oil in a frying pan (skillet) over a medium heat and shallow-fry the stuffed flowers until all the sides are golden. Drain on paper towels then place on top of the grilled vegetables. Drizzle over the dressing.

# ASSORTED SUMMER ROLLS



GỎI CUỐN

These fresh rice-paper salad rolls are ever so exquisite and a favourite among many. The more effort you put into the fillings, the bigger the rewards, although they are a great vessel for leftovers as well. Summer rolls also make the perfect ice-breaking, fun dinner party. Pack your rolls with contrasting flavours and textures: for instance, fill them with soft, silky and meaty mushrooms, married with crunchy Jerusalem artichoke. To make the most vibrant summer rolls, use a selection of these leaves. The more herbs you can get, the better the rolls become, but only using the freshest summer garden mint and coriander (cilantro) will work magically.

Makes 6
Prep time — 30–40 minutes
Cooking time — 20 minutes

For the mushroom, tofu and Jerusalem artichoke filling

10 g (⅓ oz) butter
1 teaspoon olive oil
1 small round shallot, sliced
2 garlic cloves, finely chopped
150 g (5 oz) assorted mushrooms, sliced
1 tablespoon vegetarian oyster sauce
pinch of freshly ground black pepper
200 g (7 oz) fried tofu, sliced into 6 lengths with 1 cm (½ in) thick batons (page 61)
1 teaspoon butter or rapeseed (canola) oil
60 g (2 oz) Jerusalem artichoke, sliced into matchsticks

Alternative filling options

Lemongrass Tofu (page 65); Salt and Pepper Tofu (page 62); Crispy Folded Crêpes (page 132), cut into strips; Vietnamese Dough Sticks (page 32), cut at a diagonal; Vegetable Spring Rolls (page 118), cut at a diagonal

For the salad

6 sheets of 22 cm (8⅔ in) diameter rice paper
Use approximately 20 g (¾ oz) of any of these herbs: coriander (cilantro), mint, Vietnamese balm, perilla, fish mint, Vietnamese coriander, garlic chives
6 leaves of soft lettuce or little gem lettuce
80 g (3 oz) rice vermicelli noodles, rehydrated with boiling water from the kettle until soft then drain, rinse and leave in colander

For the hoisin and peanut butter dipping sauce (page 213)

Use any filling that you would like. For the mushroom, tofu and Jerusalem artichoke filling, add the butter, oil and shallot into a frying pan (skillet) over a medium-high heat. Once the shallot starts to colour, add the garlic and fry until they both start to turn golden. Add the mushrooms with the vegetarian oyster sauce and black pepper. Stir-fry for a few minutes then add the tofu and fry until the mushrooms have softened. Set aside in a bowl to cool. Using the same frying pan on medium-high heat, add the butter and throw in the Jerusalem artichoke matchsticks. Let sit for a minute then toss and stir them for a couple of minutes until they char. Set aside in another bowl to cool.

Make the dipping sauce according to the instructions on page 213. Set aside.

Pour some cold tap water into a tray deep and large enough to dip the rice paper. Dip the paper to moisten for one second, then place it flat onto a cutting board.

If you view the round sheet of rice paper as a 'face', line up the filling where the 'mouth' would be, then add a small portion of herbs, lettuce and noodles. If you have a moist filling, place it on a lettuce leaf to prevent the paper from breaking from the moisture. Fold the two sides in (where the 'ears' would be), then fold over the bottom flap – the 'chin' – to cover the ingredients. It should look like you are making an envelope. Then, as tightly as possible, starting from the bottom, roll and push down as you go along until you have reached the top of the rice paper (the 'head').

Serve immediately with the dipping sauce, or keep the rolls in an airtight container at room temperature and serve within 2–3 hours.

# SWEET POTATO AND CELERIAC CHIPS WRAPPED IN BETEL LEAVES

LÁ LỐT CUỘN RAU CỦ

The sweetness and caramelisation of these chips are irresistible. Combine heat and aromatics with the beautiful peppery, slightly bitter betel leaf and we have a flavour explosion. When cooked, the leaves release a gorgeous cinnamon-like scent which lingers in the air and on our tastebuds. You will need skewers, which need to have been soaked in water if they are wooden.

Serves 4
Prep time — 30 minutes
Cooking time — 50 minutes

3 tablespoons rapeseed (canola) oil
200 g (7 oz) purple sweet potatoes, peeled, cut into chips
200 g (7 oz) orange sweet potatoes, peeled, cut into chips
200 g (7 oz) celeriac, peeled, cut into chips
sea salt and freshly ground black pepper
2 tablespoons Lemongrass and Chilli Oil (page 210)
100 g (3½ oz) betel leaves, de-stalked with scissors, leaving 1 cm (½ in) of stem
1 tablespoon sesame oil
2 tablespoons salted peanuts, chopped
2 tablespoons Spring Onion Oil (page 210)

Preheat a fan oven to 200°C (400°F/gas 2). Drizzle 2 tablespoons of the oil in a baking tray (pan) large enough to hold the vegetables and place it in the oven for 15 minutes.

Take out the tray and scatter the sweet potato and celeriac chips onto it; the oil should sizzle. Using tongs, very gently turn the chips to coat them with the hot oil, leaving some space between them. Season with salt and pepper. Bake for 25–30 minutes, turning halfway through.

When done, use a spatula to loosen any chips that are stuck. Drizzle the lemongrass chilli oil over the chips and coat evenly. On a cutting board, place a betel leaf shiny-side down with the stem towards you (use two leaves side by side if they are too small). Place a chip on the leaf at the stem end and roll the chip and leaf into a cigar and place flap-side down. Repeat until done and then thread three or four rolls into little short skewers.

To cook the skewers, use a hot griddle pan, a grill rack over a gas stove or a barbecue for about 2 minutes on each side.

To serve, drizzle with the sesame oil, chopped peanuts and spring onion oil. This is great with vermicelli noodle salad bowls (page 137) or a topping on a bowl of rice.

NOTE

There isn't anything that can replace the special essence of betel leaves; however, if you cannot get betel leaves, use perilla leaves, or leaves that are not too watery such as sliced rainbow chard, beetroot (beet) tops, cavolo nero, savoy cabbage.

# FOUR

# ONE-PLATE NOODLES

'*Tội nghiệp Ma Nga qua*' (Poor you, Mummy), I'd gently offer my condolences – not for eating delicious noodles, but for the melancholy of her solitude in eating from a lone plate, rather than sharing a meal with others. My mother wishes me the same sentiment whenever I am ill or sad and it has always cheered me up to be understood and acknowledged in this way.

For ease, solo-plate meals became something the whole family had, often in front of the TV. My brother and I used to have living-room discos around oursolo plates, the stereo blasting 'Everywhere' by Fleetwood Mac. Wavy noodles would hang from our mouths as we marvelled over A-ha's 'Take On Me' video, and slurping on them comforted us as we watched the penalty shoot-out between England and Germany. We began to describe lone-plate eating as 'eating the English way' and it symbolised a small connection to being British, that we too ate from plates and not little rice bowls.

When we first arrived in the UK, we lived in a small bed and breakfast for what seemed like the longest winter. We had no money and no kitchen, so we ate endless instant noodles thanks to the kettle in our room, but my mum would enhance them with all sorts of vegetables on offer at the corner shop, like slices of a carrot, torn-up iceberg lettuce, button mushrooms and so on, topped with a few squirts of Maggi which was like liquid gold. Despite our lack of resources, she still made us gorgeous bowls and plates of noodles and I continue to do the same with whatever I have available.

# SWEET POTATO NOODLES WITH ROASTED FENNEL AND SWEETHEART CABBAGE

## MIẾN XÀO CÂY TIỂU HỒI HƯƠNG NƯỚNG VÀ BẮP CẢI

This dish is incredibly delicious with crunchy and succulent vegetables and soft translucent glass noodles which soak up all the flavours of the sauce. It can be served hot or as a cold salad for quick midweek meals, as well as on special occasions.

Serves 4 as a sharing dish
Prep time — 20 minutes
Cooking time — 35–40 minutes

For the roasted fennel

1 tablespoon rapeseed (canola) oil
250 g (9 oz) fennel

For the sauce

3 bird's eye chillies, finely chopped
3 tablespoons soy sauce
2 tablespoons vegetarian oyster sauce
1½ tablespoons maple syrup
1 tablespoon lime juice
pinch of freshly ground black pepper

For the noodles

200 g (7 oz) (Korean) sweet potato noodles, soaked in boiling water for 10 minutes, covered
1 tablespoon groundnut (peanut) or avocado oil
1 teaspoon sesame oil
1 tablespoon vegetable oil
2 round shallots, sliced
2 garlic cloves, finely chopped
100 g (3½ oz) sweetheart (hispi) cabbage, thinly sliced
250 ml (8½ fl oz/1 cup) coconut water or vegetable stock
30 g (1 oz) spring onion (scallion), finely sliced

For the garnish

20 g (¾ oz) Vietnamese coriander, cut into 5 cm (2 in) pieces
50 g (1¾ oz) pistachios, cashews or peanuts, roughly chopped and lightly toasted
lots of freshly ground black pepper
shop-bought crispy chilli oil or chilli sauce (optional)

Preheat a fan oven to 200°C (400°F/gas 6). Drizzle the oil on a baking sheet and place it in the oven to heat up.

Cut the fennel into quarters then grill them on a hot griddle pan until char marks appear on all sides. When the oven is hot enough, take out the baking sheet and toss the charred fennel in the oil. Roast the fennel for 20 minutes.

In a small bowl, mix together the sauce ingredients and set aside.

Soak and drain the noodles, snip them into 15–20 cm (6–8 in) lengths using scissors and then toss with the groundnut oil, sesame oil and half of the sauce mix so that all the strands become coated.

Once the fennel is done, heat a large frying pan (skillet) or wok over a medium heat, add ½ tablespoon of the vegetable oil and fry half the shallot until golden, then add half the garlic and fry until fragrant and golden. Next, add the cabbage and half the coconut water and cook for 2 minutes. Add the roasted fennel and cook for another 2 minutes. Pour over the rest of the sauce. Stir-fry and mix together for a further minute. Set aside on a plate.

Starting again in the same pan over a medium-high heat, add the remaining vegetable oil and fry the rest of the shallot, then the garlic as above. When golden, add the noodles and fry vigorously for about 4–5 minutes, until the noodles turn soft, adding the rest of the coconut water to steam the noodles and to separate them. Then combine with the spring onion. The noodles should be wet and slippery. Remove from the heat and mix together with the fried vegetables.

Dish up onto a big platter to share and sprinkle with the Vietnamese coriander, nuts, pepper and chilli oil, if using.

NOTE

You can also use thinner glass noodles, made from mung beans or arrowroot, and fry for less time as they will cook quicker.

# CAVOLO NERO NOODLES

MÌ XÀO CẢI ĐEN

You can use any sliced greens to make this already speedy dish even faster. This is perfect to serve as cold noodles in lunch boxes or picnics. Garnish with whatever you like or just keep plain and simple.

Serves 2
Prep time — 5 minutes
Cooking time — 10 minutes

120 g (4 oz) ramen noodles
½ tablespoon ghee or cooking oil
2 shallots, finely sliced
2 garlic cloves, finely sliced
180 g (6⅓ oz) cavolo nero, sliced into 3 cm (1 in) pieces
2 tablespoons vegetarian oyster sauce
2 teaspoons Crispy Chilli Oil or Lemongrass Chilli Oil (page 210)
sprinkle of flaked almonds (optional)
½ bird's eye chilli, sliced (optional)

For the garnish (optional)

coriander (cilantro) leaves, garlic chives, Thai basil, toasted sesame seeds, nuts, nori flakes, chilli flakes, *gim* (Korean seasoned seaweed)

Cook the noodles for 3 minutes less than the packet instructions, rinse and drain in a colander. Set aside.

In a wok over a high heat, add the ghee and fry the shallot until golden, then add the garlic for a minute to release its lovely aroma. Then add the cavolo nero. Stir-fry until the leaves wilt, then add the noodles and vegetarian oyster sauce. Combine and stir-fry for about 3 minutes, then serve immediately with crispy chilli oil and a sprinkle of almond flakes (if using) and chilli (if using) plus any garnish you have available.

# COURGETTE SPAGHETTI WITH MISO AND NORI

MÌ BÍ NGÒI VỚI MISO VÀ RONG BIỂN KHÔ

So quick, so good. You're welcome!

Serves 1
Prep time — 5 minutes
Cooking time — 15 minutes

110 g (3⅔ oz) spaghetti, Size No. 5 (Barilla)
½ tablespoon sea salt
1 teaspoon ghee
1 shallot, sliced
1 large garlic clove, halved
1½ teaspoons miso
1 teaspoon soy sauce or Homemade Vegan Fish Sauce (page 193)
130 g (4½ oz) courgette (zucchini), julienned with a grater lengthways
1 large egg yolk, beaten
½ sheet of nori seaweed, cut into 5 mm (¼ in) strips with scissors
1 tablespoon toasted sesame seeds
½ teaspoon freshly ground black pepper
1 tablespoon *gim* (Korean seasoned seaweed) (optional)
chilli (hot pepper) flakes (optional)

Bring water in a saucepan to the boil and cook the spaghetti with the sea salt. Time the pasta; once it has cooked for 3 minutes, start to cook the rest.

In a frying pan (skillet) over a medium heat, add the ghee with the shallot and garlic and let it sizzle for 3 minutes until golden. Then add the miso and soy sauce with about 50 ml (1¾ fl oz) of water from the spaghetti pan. Mix well, then add the courgette and cook for a minute. Once the courgette has softened, add another 50 ml (1¾ fl oz) of pasta water and stir. Once the pasta is done, use tongs to quickly drag the spaghetti to the frying pan; you want the spaghetti to carry extra pasta water with it. Mix everything together and turn off the heat. Pour in the egg yolk and stir into the pasta with your tongs. Then add the nori strips. Stir again and serve with a generous sprinkling of sesame seeds, black pepper, *gim* (if using) and chilli flakes (if using).

NOTE

If you're making more than one portion, prep all the ingredients, and cook one portion at a time or make with two frying pans.

# CRISPY CHILLI TOFU NOODLES

MÌ XÀO VỚI ĐẬU HỦ CAY GIÒN

This is a quick and tasty meal for when you're busy but still want to eat well.

Serves 2
Prep time — 15 minutes
Cooking time — 5 minutes

150 g (5 oz) flat rice noodles, 5 mm (¼ in) diameter
½ tablespoon ghee or vegetable oil
2 round Asian shallots, roughly sliced
2 garlic cloves, sliced
50 g (1¾ oz) mangetout (snow peas), de-strung
150 g (5 oz) silken tofu
1 tablespoon Laoganma crispy chilli oil, plus extra for garnish
2 tablespoons soy sauce
1 teaspoon sesame oil (optional)
20 g (¾ oz) coriander (cilantro) leaves and/or Thai basil, coarsely chopped
zest and juice of ½ lime (optional)

Rehydrate the noodles by placing them in a bowl or container with a lid and pouring just-boiled water from the kettle over them. Cover for at least 4 minutes. Check if they are cooked and continue to cover if not. Every brand of rice noodles will vary in cooking time. When done, drain the noodles in a colander and rinse with hot tap water until the water runs clear of starch. Then place a lid on the colander to dry out and fluff up the noodles.

In a large frying pan (skillet) over a high heat, add the ghee and fry the shallot until golden, then add the garlic. Fry for a further minute then throw in the mangetout and toss for a couple of minutes until charred. Add the tofu and mash it with a wooden spoon or chopsticks. Add the crispy chilli oil, soy sauce and sesame oil, if using. Add the noodles, combine and stir-fry together for a couple of minutes, then add the coriander and/or Thai basil. Serve immediately, with lime juice squeezed over, scattered with the zest, if using, and more crispy chilli oil to your liking.

NOTES

Use any green, crunchy vegetables, bean sprouts or leafy greens you have going. This recipe lends itself well to rice noodles but if you have other noodles, feel free to use them. If you don't have silken tofu, it's fine to use a firmer variety or even a beaten egg.

If you're making more than two servings, make it in batches instead of filling your frying pan (skillet) with double the ingredients, as it will be hard to stir-fry.



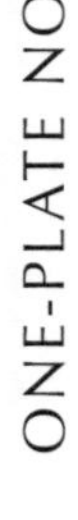

# FLAT RICE NOODLES WITH BEAN SPROUTS AND GARLIC CHIVES

HỦ TIẾU XÀO GIÁ HẸ

Deceptively plain and simple, yet hits the spot every time. Make sure the wok is hot enough to achieve the charred edges on the noodles. Garlic chives are easier to come across but, if you can forage some three-cornered leeks, they are amazing in this.

Serves 2
Prep time — 10 minutes
Cooking time — 8–10 minutes

1 tablespoon rapeseed (canola) oil
1 round shallot, roughly sliced
4 garlic cloves, sliced
400 g (14 oz) fresh flat rice noodles (*ho fun*), separated
2 tablespoons light soy sauce
½ tablespoon ghee or rapeseed (canola) oil
1 onion, sliced lengthways into 2 cm (¾ in) widths
100 g (3½ oz) bean sprouts
1 tablespoon vegetarian oyster sauce
50 g (1¾ oz) garlic chives or three-cornered leeks with flowers, snipped into 3 cm (1 in) pieces
pinch of freshly ground black pepper
chilli oil
bird's eye chillies, sliced

In a hot wok or frying pan (skillet) over a high heat, add the oil, shallot and garlic. Stir around quickly then add the noodles and soy sauce. Shake the wok and flip the noodles or use cooking chopsticks to move them around, but let them settle for a minute to get a nice char on the edges. Continue to stir-fry or flip for about 2–3 minutes until the noodles have wilted down. Set aside on a serving plate.

In the same wok, over a high heat, add the ghee. Let it melt then throw in the onion. Stir-fry and shake around until they start to char on the edges then add the bean sprouts and vegetarian oyster sauce. Mix gently, then add the garlic chives. Cook for a couple of minutes, then layer on top of the noodles on the plate. Sprinkle over the black pepper and serve immediately with an option of chilli oil and sliced chillies.

NOTE

Feel free to use rehydrated rice noodles if fresh ones are unavailable.

# WINTER MELON STIR-FRY WITH TOFU AND GLASS NOODLES

MIẾN XÀO BÍ ĐAO VÀ ĐẬU HỦ

Simple vegetable stir-fries are nice, but sometimes they need jazzing up a little with slippery glass noodles, which soak up all the flavours in the most delicious way.

Serves 2–4 as a sharing dish
Prep time — 15 minutes
Cooking time — 25 minutes

300 g (10½ oz) medium-firm tofu, sliced into 1 cm (½ in) x 4 cm (1½ in) pieces
1 tablespoon rapeseed (canola) oil
4 garlic cloves, sliced
1–2 bird's eye chillies, finely chopped (optional)
250 g (9 oz) winter melon, peeled and seeds removed, thinly sliced
100 g (3½ oz) fine glass noodles soaked in cold water for 10 minutes, drained
250 ml (8½ fl oz/1 cup) aloe vera juice or coconut water
1½ tablespoons vegetarian oyster sauce
1 tablespoon soy sauce, Yondu vegetable umami or Homemade Vegan Fish Sauce (page 193)
pinch of freshly ground black pepper
1 tablespoon shop-bought crispy chilli oil or Lemongrass Chilli Oil (page 210) (optional)
1 bird's eye chilli, sliced (optional)

Prepare and fry the tofu as directed on page 61, and set aside.

Bring a large wok or frying pan (skillet) to a high heat. Add the oil, garlic and chillies, if using, and fry until the garlic starts to turn golden. Throw in the winter melon and leave to sizzle for a minute or until the bottoms have turned slightly brown before adding the noodles and tofu strips.

Toss and stir-fry for a minute, then add half the aloe vera juice, the vegetarian oyster sauce and soy sauce. Stir-fry to combine all the elements together for another minute. If it looks dry, add aloe vera juice as needed. Once the noodles and vegetables have wilted and are embracing each other, remove from the heat and serve immediately on a large sharing plate with the black pepper and crispy chilli oil (if using) or chilli, if you would like.

NOTE

You can also use sliced purple sprouting broccoli, kohlrabi, kimchi, marrow, courgette (zucchini), asparagus, green beans and bean sprouts.



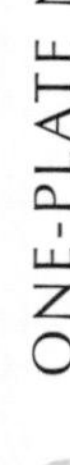

# QUICK AND LAZY DRENCHED COLD NOODLES

MÌ TRỘN

This is a delicious and easy way to prepare a super-fast lunch on busy days and great to use up things you have sitting around in the refrigerator and storecupboard. Make sure your garlic and shallot oil is nice and hot. I like to use a cold-pressed rapeseed oil but feel free to use vegetable or sunflower oil. If cooking for a crowd, prep all the bowls and only do the final pouring of hot oil when ready to serve.

Serves 2
Prep time — 15 minutes
Cooking time — 10 minutes

100 g (3½ oz) flat rice noodles, or cooked ramen noodles
1 small round shallot, sliced
2 tablespoons rapeseed (canola) oil
2 teaspoons toasted sesame seeds
2 tablespoons crispy chilli oil (Laoganma or Pippy Eats)
2 tablespoons light soy sauce
1½ teaspoons maple syrup
1 teaspoon black vinegar or cider vinegar
2 teaspoons sesame oil
handful of coriander (cilantro) leaves (around 20 g (¾ oz))
30 g (1 oz) garlic chives (optional)
2 garlic cloves, roughly sliced
2 teaspoons hot Maggi liquid seasoning (optional)

Rehydrate the noodles by placing them in a bowl or container with a lid and pouring just-boiled water from the kettle over them. Cover for at least 4 minutes. Check if they are cooked and continue to cover if not. When done, drain in a colander and rinse with hot tap water until the water runs clear of starch. Then place a lid on the colander to dry out. This fluffs up the noodles.

In a small frying pan (skillet) over a medium heat, add the shallot and oil, and gently cook for about 3 minutes before turning off the heat.

Between two small noodle bowls, divide the sesame seeds, crispy chilli oil, soy sauce, maple syrup, black vinegar, sesame oil, coriander and garlic chives, if using.

Going back to the pan of oil and shallots, turn the heat to high and add the garlic. Cook for 2 minutes until golden and the oil is bubbling. Then pour the hot garlic and shallot oil into each of the prepared bowls, before adding the noodles.

Serve immediately; the fun is mixing it all up with chopsticks as you eat. Feel free to squirt over hot Maggi liquid seasoning, if using, and further dress your bowl with your favourite condiments.

# FRIED BÁNH CANH NOODLES WITH PURPLE SPROUTING BROCCOLI

## BÁNH CANH XÀO BẮP CẢI TÍ HON TÍM

I especially love the *bánh canh* noodles here, because they have such a satisfying bite. Use any vegetables you like, and think about crunchy textures to contrast with the silky noodles. Quick stir-fries like these are what dreams are made of. Fantastic with a fried egg.

Serves 2
Prep time — 10 minutes
Cooking time — 15 minutes

400 g (14 oz) Homemade Bánh Canh Noodles (page 198) or 2 x 200 g (7 oz) packets of fresh udon noodles
2 tablespoons perilla sauce or 1 tablespoon soy sauce or Homemade Vegan Fish Sauce (page 193)
1 tablespoon maple syrup
1 teaspoon cider vinegar or black vinegar
3 tablespoons rapeseed (canola) oil
2 small round shallots, sliced
1 tablespoon vegetarian oyster sauce or ½ tablespoon black bean sauce
pinch of freshly ground black pepper
4 garlic cloves, finely chopped
100 g (3½ oz) purple sprouting broccoli
50 g (1¾ oz) bean sprouts
1 red chilli, sliced (optional)
2 tablespoons *gim* (Korean seasoned seaweed)
Japanese chilli flakes (optional)

Cook the homemade noodles in boiling water or submerge the udon in boiling water for 5 minutes, then drain and rinse well. Set aside in a colander.

In a small bowl, mix together the perilla sauce, maple syrup and vinegar. Set this seasoning mix aside.

On a medium-high heat, in a wok or large frying pan (skillet), add 2 tablespoons of the oil and the shallot. Stir-fry until golden then add the noodles. Count to 40 to let the noodles sear, then gently flip them with a thin spatula and count to 40 again to sear the other side. Drizzle the noodles with vegetarian oyster sauce and season with the black pepper. Stir-fry gently for 2–3 minutes then set aside onto a platter or divide onto plates.

In the same pan, add the remaining oil, bring to a high heat and add the garlic. As soon as it turns golden, add the purple sprouting broccoli. Let it sit for 20 seconds, then splash in 50 ml (1¾ fl oz) of water to steam the broccoli, add the seasoning mix and stir-fry for 2 minutes before adding the bean sprouts and red chilli slices, if using, and stir-fry for another minute until the bean sprouts have wilted a little. Remove from the heat and dish up on top of the noodles. With a pair of chopsticks, weave the stir-fry into the noodles and then sprinkle with gim and Japanese chilli flakes, if using. Serve immediately.

# CRISPY NOODLES WITH ALL THE BROCCOLI

## MÌ XÀO DÒN

Crispy noodles will always remind me of my late stepfather, Chú Tùng, whom my mum loved very much. Every weekend, he stood by the stove with chopsticks, deep-frying noodle nests to perfection as a treat for all of us. A juicy stir-fry of colourful vegetables rests on top of the crunchy nests of noodles and the gravy coats the noodles.

Serves 2 (if you want to cook more, please do so in batches of two)
Prep time — 20 minutes
Cooking time — 15 minutes

2 x 80 g (3 oz) bundles of Crispy Noodles (page 200)

For the seasoning

1 teaspoon fermented tofu, mashed or miso
1½ tablespoons Homemade Vegan Fish Sauce (page 193)
1 tablespoon vegetarian oyster sauce
1 tablespoon maple syrup
½ tablespoon rice wine vinegar
1 teaspoon sesame oil
1 level tablespoon cornflour (cornstarch)
200 ml (7 fl oz/scant 1 cup) coconut water or unseasoned vegetable broth

For the stir-fry

1 tablespoon rapeseed (canola) oil
2 small round shallots, sliced
2 garlic cloves, sliced
100 g (3½ oz) Tenderstem or purple sprouting broccoli, sliced into bite-size lengths at a diagonal
50 g (1¾ oz) baby corn, halved lengthways
50 g (1¾ oz) carrot, julienned
150 g (5 oz) medium-firm tofu, fried until golden then sliced into thin strips (page 61), or Vegan Vietnamese Sausages (page 117) or mushrooms
150 g (5 oz) Chinese broccoli (kai lan) leaves or cime di rapa (broccoli rabe) leaves, sliced into bite-size lengths at a diagonal
50 g (1¾ oz) radicchio, sliced into 1 cm (½ in) lengths
50 g (1¾ oz) spring onions (scallions), sliced lengthways
1 mild red chilli, sliced
freshly ground black pepper
fresh herbs to garnish: coriander (cilantro), Vietnamese coriander or fish mint

Fry the crispy noodles and set aside on a platter or individual dinner plates.

Mix the fermented tofu, vegan fish sauce, vegetarian oyster sauce, maple syrup, vinegar and sesame oil together in a small bowl. Set the seasoning mix aside. In another small bowl, combine the cornflour with 50 ml (1¾ fl oz) of the coconut water until free of lumps. Set the cornflour mix aside.

In a wok or large frying pan (skillet) over a medium-high heat, add the oil and fry the shallot until golden, then add the garlic. Wait until the aroma is released and the garlic starts to turn golden, then add the broccoli, baby corn, carrot and tofu. Stir-fry for 30 seconds, then add half of the remaining coconut water followed by the broccoli leaves and stir-fry until the leaves have wilted by half.

Pour over the seasoning mix and the rest of the coconut water, combine and stir-fry for a minute. The juices should be coming out of the vegetables and the seasoning should be sizzling. Add the radicchio, spring onion and chilli. In a circular motion, pour over a third of the cornflour mix and stir-fry for a minute. Pour over another third and stir-fry for a minute until the juices start to thicken and pour over the remainder and stir-fry for a final minute.

Dish up the stir-fried vegetables on top of the crispy noodles. Season with black pepper and garnish with herbs of your choice.

NOTES

You can play around with the toppings you use in this dish, but make sure there are leaves contrasting with crunchy vegetables and always think about texture and colour. You can use all sorts of greens such as mugwort leaves, Chinese violets, pak choi (bok choi), spinach, mustard leaves. For crunchy vegetables, use kohlrabi, daikon, lotus root, green beans, runner beans, sugar snap peas and mangetout (snow peas).

# FIVE

# CRAVINGS

'*Thèm muốn gì*?' (What food do you crave?) My mother always smiles when she says that. She catches a few requests that we throw into her net and, like magic, a feast appears. My mum pours her heart into everything she cooks because when you *thèm* (crave) something, it feels like an emergency that she must solve.

Every day, I crave, *thèm*. The weather, the seasons, the light, the mood… makes me crave my grandmother's wonderful lemongrass broth (page 148), crispy coconut crêpes stuffed with salad (page 122), an extravagant *bánh mì* (page 127) or a bowl of coconut rice pudding (page 171). We came from such a long history of hunger, historically and personally, that the fear of not eating is instilled in me. Perhaps this is where eating for fun fills the void. The act of cooking and gathering is also a thirst – being separated from my grandmothers, aunties and uncles when we left Vietnam still lacerates my heart, hence why I compensated with hosting 12 years of the most joyful supper clubs in my home every weekend until my bones finally yearned to rest.

I travel to Sài Gòn as often as I can, to reconnect with my cousins from my mother's side of the family. As soon as I step off the flight into the blast of Sài Gòn heat, I am offered the coldest of freshly-pressed sugar cane juice, topped with a hint of kumquat. I always feel the love and affection of my family caress me ever so tenderly via their filling me up on the most delicious of food and drink. We hit my favourite *hủ tiếu* (page 146) vendor on a corner of a busy road and wait patiently for the longest 2 minutes in the scorching, humid heat, for the aunt to blanch her homemade egg noodles with wontons, bean sprouts and garlic chives, fill the bowl with broth and top it off with fried garlic. I dip a long fried dough stick (page 32) into my bowl to soak up all the juices from the broth and eat ravenously. I arrive, home.

On our way to visit markets and seaside resorts, we take pauses on the Honda to buy sundried banana rice-paper cake, *bánh patê sô* (page 28), *xôi gấc* (sweet gourd red sticky rice), dragon fruit, jackfruit, rambutans and everywhere we go, I only have to close my eyes and taste the flavours and I would be a five-year-old girl again, scraping flesh from a young coconut with a long dessert spoon. Everything I have ever longed for is there.

# VEGAN VIETNAMESE SAUSAGE

CHẢ LỤA CHAY

Vietnamese sausages are wrapped in banana leaves then steamed. Their delicate fragrance is absorbed by the sausages and this makes them really special. The sliced sausages are great as toppings on noodle soups, stir-fries or rice. They also make excellent gifts as they are already wrapped. Note that it may be worth making double the amount and freezing some for future use, as it takes a while to make these. Delicious refried in spring onion oil.

Makes 2 x 20 x 3 cm (8 x 1 in)
Soaking time — 1 hour
Prep time — 40 minutes–1 hour
Cooking time — 2 hours

- 200 g (7 oz) dried beancurd strips, soaked 1 hour in warm water
- 1 tablespoon sea salt
- 1 tablespoon vegetable oil
- 55 g (2 oz) white part of spring onions (scallions) or leek, finely sliced
- 2 tablespoons Homemade Vegan Fish Sauce (page 193) or soy sauce
- 1½ teaspoons black peppercorns, crushed
- 2 heaped teaspoons nutritional yeast
- 2 teaspoons sugar
- 6 banana-leaf pieces, cut into 30 cm (12 in) squares (or kitchen foil), cleaned

Drain the soaking beancurd and then trim off and discard any hard edges. Rinse well then snip the beancurd into 5 cm (2 in) pieces. Place in a saucepan, add the salt and cover with boiling water from the kettle. Bring to a boil and then turn the heat down to medium and simmer the beancurd for 10 minutes.

In a small frying pan (skillet), heat the oil over a medium-low heat, gently fry the spring onion until golden. Scoop out the spring onion with a spider or small sieve to drain off the excess oil and set aside.

Place a muslin (cheesecloth) into a colander and drain the beancurd. Wait until it is cool enough to handle, then wring out the water and place the beancurd into a large bowl. Add the vegan fish sauce, crushed black pepper, nutritional yeast, sugar and fried spring onions. Mix well.

Place half the mixture in a plastic food bag or paper sandwich bag and tightly press out any air. Then, as tightly and securely as you can, roll it into a sausage of about 6–8 cm (2⅓–3 in) width. Repeat with the other half, then sit the sausages in the freezer for 1 hour.

Take three banana-leaf pieces. Place one piece, shiny-side down on your worktop or cutting board, then another on top of that piece with the grain going the opposite way, and then the third shiny-side down. Repeat with the other 3 banana-leaf pieces.

Take the sausages out from the freezer and remove the wrapping. Lay one sausage at the bottom of one set of banana leaves and, as tightly as possible, roll it up and secure with an elastic band. Tie the parcels using butcher's string, removing the elastic bands.

Steam for 1 hour, making sure your steamer does not run out of water (top up if necessary). In an electric steamer, press the steam button for 40 minutes with about 400 ml (13 fl oz/ generous 1½ cups) water (sealing mode).

Let the sausage parcels cool to room temperature before opening. Slice to 5 mm–1 cm (¼–½ in) thickness.

# VEGETABLE SPRING ROLLS

CHẢ GIÒ CHAY

If you want to please a crowd, Vietnamese fried spring rolls will do the trick. I use an array of vegetables to get the perfect combination of crunch and crispiness. I love using frozen Chinese spring-roll wrappers: they are easy to handle, freeze really well and fry beautifully from frozen. You're welcome to use rice paper which is typically Vietnamese. Make sure you roll as tightly as possible so that the rolls don't split as they are being fried.

Makes 30–50
Prep time — 1 hour–1 hour 30 minutes
Cooking time — 50 minutes–1 hour 30 minutes

For the filling

30 g (1 oz) split mung beans
30 g (1 oz) split red lentils
50 g (1¾ oz) glass noodles
110 g (3⅔ oz) asparagus, sliced, quartered lengthways into 5 cm (2 in) strips
140 g (scant 5 oz) Jerusalem artichokes (or tinned water chestnuts), peeled and julienned
100 g (3½ oz) leek, sliced into 5 mm (¼ in) pieces
120 g (4 oz) white cabbage, finely sliced
150 g (5 oz) parsnips, peeled and julienned
150 g (5 oz) carrots, peeled and julienned
70 g (2½ oz) bean sprouts
1 tablespoon maple syrup
1 tablespoon mushroom seasoning powder
pinch of coarse black pepper
2 pinches of sea salt
2 spring onions (scallions), green and white parts, finely sliced
2 garlic cloves, finely chopped

For wrapping

2 tablespoons cooking oil
50 spring roll wrappers, size 10 cm (4 in) or 12 cm (4¾ in)
sunflower or vegetable oil, for deep-frying

For the garnish

1 lettuce, leaves separated
an array of herbs of choice: coriander (cilantro), Vietnamese coriander, mint, perilla
a choice of dipping sauces (page 212), but I recommend the traditional nước chấm

Soak the mung beans, split lentils and glass noodles together in cold water for 20 minutes, then drain well. Snip the noodles into 3 cm (1 in) lengths.

Combine all of the filling ingredients together in a large bowl. Mix it well with your hands or tongs so that it soaks in all the seasoning. Place the oil in a small bowl.

Place one of the square wrappers on a clean work surface, rotated like a diamond. Place a small 'sausage' of filling (about 1 tablespoon) on the bottom half of the 'diamond'.

Fold in the two sides over the 'sausage', as if you are making an envelope, and then fold up the bottom flap. Using your fingers to secure the roll from the bottom, push forward and tuck in as you roll towards the top of the paper making sure it is tight. Seal the roll with a touch of the oil on the tip, using your finger or a pastry brush. Place on a clean and dry baking sheet or plate, flap-side down. Repeat until done but place your made rolls side by side, as stacking will break them.

At this point, you can freeze the rolls and cook from frozen or cook immediately.

Put a pan or wok with 5 cm (2 in) of oil on a medium-high heat until it reaches about 140°C (275°F). If you don't have a thermometer, the oil is ready if you dip a chopstick in and it sizzles and bubbles. Add 4–5 spring rolls (do not crowd the pan or they will stick together) and deep-fry for 4–5 minutes or until golden brown. If cooking from frozen, add 3–4 minutes to the cooking time.

Serve immediately with a platter of lettuce and herbs with a dipping sauce, and/or snip each roll into 3 diagonal pieces and serve on vermicelli noodle salad bowls (page 137).

NOTES

You can add whatever vegetables you like, but avoid any with a high water content, such as mushrooms, Chinese cabbage or courgettes (zucchini), without cooking them first and squeezing out the water, as this will result in soggy spring rolls. Instead of frying, you can brush the rolls with oil and bake them for 10 minutes in a fan oven preheated to 200°C (400°F/gas 6), turning after 5 minutes. If you use rice paper, fry them after you've made about 12.

# SAVOURY PANCAKE BITES

BÁNH KHỌT CHAY

These delicious little bites serve as great starters and snacks, or make lots as part of a feast. Each mini pancake is a teaser for all the goodness of vegetables. The combination here plays with crunch and softness. Serve with little gem lettuce and lots of herbs.

Serves 4
Soaking time — 1 hour
Prep time — 20 minutes
Cooking time — 30 minutes–1 hour

For the batter

135 g (4¾ oz/generous ¾ cup) Asian rice flour
40 g (1½ oz/⅓ cup) cornflour (cornstarch)
½ teaspoon ground turmeric
¾ teaspoon garlic powder
generous pinch of sea salt
260 ml (8¾ fl oz/generous 1 cup) coconut milk
260 ml (8¾ fl oz/generous 1 cup) sparkling water
3 spring onions (scallions), green and white parts, thinly sliced
7 tablespoons cooking oil

For the filling

1 tablespoon cooking oil
3 garlic cloves, sliced
60 g (2 oz) split mung beans, soaked 30 minutes–1 hour, then rinsed and drained
100 g (3½ oz) fine green beans, sliced into 5 mm (¼ in) circles
80 g (3 oz) oyster mushrooms, sliced into 5 mm (¼ in) pieces
3 chestnut mushrooms, sliced into 5 mm (¼ in) pieces
1 tablespoon soy sauce
1 tablespoon ponzu or rice vinegar
1 tablespoon maple syrup
6 okra, sliced into 5 mm (¼ in) circles

For the tahini soy dressing

4 tablespoons soy sauce
1 tablespoon tahini
juice of ¼ lime or lemon
1 teaspoon maple syrup

To serve

little gem lettuce and/or chicory
coriander (cilantro), mint, Thai basil or any variety of Vietnamese herbs (choose at least one)

In a mixing bowl, add the rice flour, cornflour, turmeric, garlic powder, salt and coconut milk. Whisk well together until there are no more lumps, then rest the batter for about an hour.

In a wok or frying pan (skillet), add the cooking oil and garlic over a medium heat. When the garlic starts to take colour, add the mung beans and green beans. Stir-fry for 3 minutes, then add the mushrooms, soy sauce, ponzu and maple syrup. Stir-fry for another 3 minutes until the mushrooms have softened and set aside.

Mix the dressing ingredients together and decant into individual dipping bowls.

After the batter has rested, add the sparkling water and spring onion and mix well together. Pour the batter into a jug.

Heat a takoyaki grill pan over a medium-high heat. After a couple of minutes, hover your hand 10 cm (4 in) over the pan. If it feels too hot for you to hold it there, it is ready. Add ¼ teaspoon of the cooking oil into each hole. Mix the batter again to ensure even consistency, before pouring it into the wells, leaving about 5 mm (¼ in) at the top of each well. Garnish each *bánh khọt* with a level teaspoon of the filling and decorate with a slice or two of okra on top.

Cover the takoyaki grill pan with a lid. If you don't have a square one that fits, fashion a piece of kitchen foil to cover. Cook for 6–9 minutes depending on how hot your stove is. The bánh khọt bottoms should be brown and crispy.

Remove the bánh khọt from the pan with a spoon onto serving plates and repeat with the rest of the batter and filling.

To serve, feel free to use nuts, seeds and condiments you have in the storecupboard, such as almond flakes, *gim* or seaweed. Just make sure the contents are sliced up, small to the bite and crunchy.

To eat, place a lettuce leaf onto the palm of your hand, layer it with plenty of herbs and a bánh khọt. Spoon over a little dressing and enjoy.

NOTE

If you do not have a takoyaki pan, preheat the oven to 220°C (425°F/gas 7), place a fairy cake tin with a 2 mm (⅛ in) layer of cooking oil to heat up for 15 minutes, then pour 2 cm (¾ in) of batter into the wells, before adding the filling. Bake for about 20 minutes.

# CRISPY VEGETABLE CRÊPES

BÁNH XÈO CHAY

These marvellous crêpes are usually enjoyed 'playfully' in the evenings. I've given them a green twist by adding spinach to the batter and packing them with crunchy green vegetables. You need a good non-stick frying pan and rice flour from an Asian store.

Serves 4–5 (makes approx. 12 x 20 cm (8 in) crêpes)
Prep time — 30 minutes
Cooking time — 1 hour

For the salad

any lettuce leaves
selection of Vietnamese herbs (page 14)

For the dipping sauce

2½ tablespoons marmalade
3 teaspoons English mustard
2½ tablespoons soy sauce
juice of ¾ lime (about 2 tablespoons)
2 bird's eye chillies, sliced

For the batter

150 g (5 oz) frozen spinach, defrosted for 1 hour
200 ml (7 fl oz/scant 1 cup) water
200 g (7 oz/generous 1 cup) rice flour
400 ml (13 fl oz/generous 1½ cups) coconut milk
200 ml (7 fl oz/scant 1 cup) cold sparkling water
1 spring onion (scallion), thinly sliced
2 tablespoons nutritional yeast
½ teaspoon sea salt or mushroom seasoning

For the filling

150 ml (5 fl oz/scant ⅔ cup) rapeseed (canola) oil
3 small round shallots, sliced
1 courgette (zucchini), julienned
100 g (3½ oz) kale, stem removed, thinly sliced
100 g (3½ oz) bean sprouts
50 g (1¾ oz) garlic chives, cut into 4 cm (1½ in) strips
2 tablespoons capers
100 g (3½ oz) kimchi, sliced (optional)

Wash and dry the salad leaves and herbs and set them aside. Mix the dipping sauce ingredients together and decant into individual bowls.

To make the crêpe batter, put the frozen spinach into a blender with the water and blend until smooth. In a mixing bowl, mix together the rice flour, coconut milk, sparkling water, spring onion, nutritional yeast and salt. Add the spinach blend and whisk together until smooth and the consistency of single cream.

Place all your prepped filling ingredients near the stove. Heat 1 tablespoon of the oil in a frying pan (skillet) over a medium-high heat and fry a few slices of shallot until golden.

Using a shallow ladle, mix the crêpe batter well to ensure even consistency and pour in a thin layer, swirling the pan to get it covered to the edges. Add a handful of the courgette, kale, bean sprouts and chives, then cover the pan with the lid. Keep the steam in and allow to cook for 2 minutes.

Remove the lid, dot with the capers and scatter the kimchi (if using) around. Cook for a further 1–2 minutes, making sure the crêpe is crisp and golden. Fold the crêpe in half, serve or set aside. Repeat this process to make the rest of the bánh xèo.

To eat, gather a lettuce leaf on the palm of your hand and fill it up with an abundance of herbs. Break off a piece of bánh xèo and place it onto your herb-filled lettuce leaf. Roll up the package into a cigar, dip it in the sauce and tuck in.

NOTES

If you want to make these ahead, set them on a baking tray (pan) side by side. When ready to serve, preheat a fan oven to 230°C (450°F/gas 8) and warm the bánh xèo for 5 minutes.

Add whatever vegetables you have, but make sure you slice them thinly so that there is crunch but not too much work chewing.

# ASPARAGUS RICE-NOODLE ROLLS WITH MUSHROOMS AND PUMPKIN

BÁNH CUỐN NHÂN NẤM MĂNG TÂY VÀ BÍ ĐỎ

My Aunt dì Út still lives in the old house by the seaside where my late grandfather had a fish sauce farm. She likes to sit among the enormous abandoned clay vats with a steaming drum to make the most delicious steamed rice-noodle rolls known as *bánh cuốn*. Her bánh cuốn are filled with fried shallots and spring onion, served alongside a beautiful sweet and sour fish sauce.

Serves 4–6 (makes approx. 24)
Prep time — 40 minutes
Cooking time — 1 hour–1 hour 30 minutes

For the batter

100 g (3½ oz) tapioca starch
300 g (10½ oz/1¾ cups) Asian rice flour
1 teaspoon cornflour (cornstarch)
1 litre (34 fl oz/4 cups) water
pinch of sea salt
1 teaspoon mushroom seasoning powder or sea salt
1 teaspoon vegetable oil
2 spring onions (scallions), green and white parts, finely chopped
80 g (3 oz) asparagus, sliced into fine 3 mm (⅛ in) rings
2 tablespoons cooking oil
Soy, Tahini and Crispy Chilli Oil (page 213)

For the filling

300 g (10½ oz) Delica or kabocha pumpkin, skin on, sliced into wedges
1 tablespoon rapeseed (canola) oil
2 small round shallots, finely diced
70 g (2½ oz) leek, finely sliced
200 g (7 oz) any mushrooms, finely sliced
150 g (5 oz) Jerusalem artichoke, julienned
1 tablespoon vegetarian oyster sauce
freshly ground black pepper
1½ tablespoons coconut water or aloe vera juice

For the garnish

2 tablespoons vegetable or avocado oil
Crispy Shallots (page 208)
Thai basil, finely sliced
coriander (cilantro) leaves, roughly chopped

Mix the batter ingredients in a large bowl, except for the spring onion, asparagus and oils.

Prepare the chilli oil by mixing it altogether in a bowl.

Preheat a fan oven to 190°C (375°F/gas 5) and roast the pumpkin for 25–30 minutes. Set aside to cool. Peel off the skin and cut the pumpkin into 1 cm (½ in) cubes.

Heat the oil in a frying pan (skillet) over a medium-low heat and fry the shallots and leek until just becoming translucent. Turn the heat up high, then add the mushroom and Jerusalem artichoke. Season with vegetarian oyster sauce and pepper, and cook for 3 minutes. Add the coconut water to steam the vegetables. Cook for a further 3 minutes and leave to rest.

Add the spring onion and asparagus to the batter. Bring the frying pan (skillet) to a medium heat and, using a pastry brush, lightly oil the pan with the cooking oil to cover the surface.

Stir the bowl of batter well before use as the flour and water will separate. Using a utility spoon, add in 40 ml (1⅓ fl oz/2½ tablespoons) of the batter to cover the surface of the pan, swirling the pan quickly to keep the batter thin. Add a little more if needed. Cover the pan with a lid for about 1 minute on a gas hob and 2 minutes on electric hob; the batter should turn opaque and should not crisp up. Flip the pan over onto a lightly oiled plastic cutting board to remove the cooked noodle sheet. The rougher side should be facing upwards.

Sprinkle a level tablespoon of the filling along the bottom of the noodle sheet. Scatter the pumpkin cubes along the filling. Using a spatula, flip the bottom up and roll the noodle sheet up to the top till it forms a roll. Place on a dish. Using a pastry brush, lightly brush the bánh cuốn with the vegetable oil. Repeat.

Garnish with crispy shallots, Thai basil and coriander. Drizzle a little chilli oil over the bánh cuốn.

Serve immediately or at room temperature within a couple of hours. Alternatively, reheat in a steamer or microwave for a minute.

# OMELETTE BÁNH MÌ

BÁNH MÌ TRỨNG

One of the most iconic Vietnamese dishes is the French-inspired *bánh mì*: a fresh, crispy yet fluffy baguette filled with the most captivating flavours and textures.

Serves 4
Prep time — 15 minutes
Cooking time — 5 minutes

2 French or 4 foot-long Vietnamese baguettes

For the spring onion omelette

4 eggs, beaten
2 spring onions (scallions), sliced
pinch of freshly ground black pepper
1 teaspoon caster (superfine) sugar (optional)
1 tablespoon soy sauce
1 tablespoon vegetable oil
2 round shallots, finely chopped

Required fillings

butter, for spreading
coriander (cilantro) sprigs
mint leaves
cucumber, sliced into thin lengths
Instant Carrot and Daikon Pickle (page 204)
bird's eye chillies, thinly sliced at a diagonal
Coriander Pesto (page 208)

Optional additions

Vegan Vietnamese Sausage (page 117)
Salt and Pepper Tofu (page 62)
Maggi liquid seasoning
mayonnaise
chilli sauce

Beat the eggs with the spring onion, pepper, sugar (if using) and soy sauce. Heat the oil in a frying pan (skillet) over a medium heat and brown off the shallots, then pour on the egg mixture to make the omelette, turning once one side is brown. This should take no longer than a few minutes. Remove from the heat and cut into long strips.

Slit your baguette in half along one side so that it opens like a book. Pull out the soft bread inside (enjoy as a chef's treat with butter or save for Banana Bread Layer Cake on page 180) to leave plenty of room for the filling.

Butter your baguette or spread it with coriander pesto. Stuff with a layer of all the required bánh mì fillings, then the omelette strips. Serve immediately otherwise the bread will steam up and become soggy or wait for the omelette to cool down before adding. Add Maggi liquid seasoning, mayo or chilli sauce and enjoy.

# TURMERIC AND DILL TOFU

CHẢ CÁ LÃ VỌNG CHAY

Mimicking the flavours of Vietnamese dill fish cakes, this goes well with fluffy, steamed jasmine rice or on a vermicelli noodle salad (page 137).

Serves 2 or 4 as a side dish
Prep time — 5 minutes
Cooking time — 30 minutes

200 g (7 oz) banana shallots, cut into thirds
400 g (14 oz) medium-firm tofu
4 tablespoons neutral cooking oil
1 small round Asian shallot, sliced
2 garlic cloves, roughly sliced
1 tablespoon vegetarian oyster sauce
1 tablespoon soy sauce
½ teaspoon mushroom seasoning powder or 2 tablespoon nutritional yeast
1 teaspoon ground turmeric
1 teaspoon agave or maple syrup
6 bird's eye or other chillies, whole
2 teaspoons fermented tofu
100 ml (3½ fl oz/scant ½ cup) coconut water
30 g (1 oz) dill, roughly chopped
black or pink peppercorns, crushed
juice of ¼ lime

Heat a frying pan (skillet) over a medium heat, then place the shallot flat-side down and char for about 3–5 minutes until the edges have blackened. Remove from the heat and wipe the pan with paper towels.

Cut the tofu into 1 cm (½ in) thick rectangles and pat dry. In the same pan over a medium heat, add 2 tablespoons of the oil, and fry tofu for about 8 minutes on each side or until golden, then set aside on paper towels.

In a saucepan, heat the remaining oil over a medium heat, add the shallot and garlic and cook until golden, then add the fried tofu. Gently mix in the vegetarian oyster sauce, soy sauce, mushroom seasoning powder, turmeric and agave syrup. Gently toss and stir, then add the charred shallot and whole chillies, but do not break them (unless you love things super-hot). Let it sizzle for 2 minutes.

Meanwhile, in a small bowl, mash the fermented tofu with the coconut water and add to the stir-fry, toss and stir for about 3–5 minutes then add most of the dill. Stir-fry for a minute and turn off the heat.

Serve immediately scattered with the rest of the dill, and season with pepper and the lime.

# KING OYSTER MUSHROOM AND TURMERIC RICE

CƠM GÀ HỘI AN CHAY

This is a recipe from my mum, who's always trying to cut down on meat and be at one with plants. It is so delicious, like a version of Hainanese chicken rice, which king oyster mushrooms (called 'chicken thigh mushrooms' in Vietnamese) mimic rather well. Every component supports the perfect balance.

Serves 4
Prep time — 30 minutes
Cooking time — 35 minutes

For the turmeric rice

1 tablespoon vegetable oil
1 small shallot, finely sliced
1 garlic clove, finely chopped
300 g (10½ oz/1½ cups) jasmine rice, washed and drained three times
1 tablespoon nutritional yeast
¼ teaspoon sea salt
¼ teaspoon ground turmeric
500 ml (17 fl oz/2 cups) water or Homemade Vegetable Stock (page 196)

For the pickled onions

1 red onion, sliced thinly
1 tablespoon caster (superfine) sugar
¼ teaspoon freshly ground black pepper
1½ tablespoons cider vinegar

For the ginger dipping sauce

40 g (1½ oz) fresh ginger root, peeled, finely chopped
1 garlic clove, finely chopped
½ red chilli or chillies of choice, finely chopped
2 tablespoons soy sauce or Homemade Vegan Fish Sauce (page 193)

For the mushrooms

1 tablespoon vegetable oil
2 small shallots, finely sliced
1 garlic clove, finely chopped
470 g (1 lb ½ oz) king oyster mushrooms, sliced into 5 mm (¼ in) lengths
1 teaspoon sea salt
½ teaspoon freshly ground black pepper
½ teaspoon sesame oil
2 tablespoons water
1 tablespoon vegetarian oyster sauce

For the garnish

30 g (1 oz) Vietnamese coriander leaves or coriander (cilantro) sprigs
10 cm (4 in) cucumber, thinly sliced diagonally (optional)
1 tomato, thinly sliced (optional)

Heat the oil in a saucepan over a medium heat and fry the shallot and garlic for 4 minutes until golden. Then add the rice and mix together. Sprinkle over the nutritional yeast, salt and turmeric. Mix well together, then add the water. Cover and cook over a medium-low heat for 2 minutes until the broth has been absorbed into the rice, then turn the heat down to low and cook with the lid securely on to let the steam do its work for a further 15–18 minutes. Turn off the heat and let it rest with the lid still on for 5–10 minutes. Fluff up the rice with a rice paddle or woodenspoon. Keep the lid on.

Mix the red onion, caster sugar, pepper and vinegar in a bowl and leave to pickle.

Combine all the dipping sauce ingredients together, either by hand-chopping or crushing in a pestle and mortar or blender. Decant into individual dipping bowls.

For the mushrooms, heat the oil in a large frying pan (skillet) over a medium-high heat. Add the shallot and fry until golden, then add the garlic. Let it sizzle and release its aromas then add the mushroom. Stir well together then add the salt, pepper and sesame oil. Combine before adding the water to steam the mushroom. Then add the vegetarian oyster sauce and stir-fry for another 5 minutes.

To serve, plate up the rice with the mushroom on top or at the side, garnish with the Vietnamese coriander, pickled onions and cucumber and tomatoes, if using. Serve with the ginger dipping sauce on the side.

# PUMPKIN AND CHICKPEA CURRY

BÍ NẤU CÀ RI

Spicy dishes like curries are found on the all-day breakfast menu in Vietnam because spice wakes up the senses. Traditionally enjoyed with a fresh crusty baguette to mop up all the juices, this also makes a great midweek supper as well as a dinner party main course with steamed jasmine rice. Be gentle with the pumpkin pieces as they will break easily if they are overcooked.

Serves 4
Prep time — 20 minutes
Cooking time — 40 minutes

1½ tablespoons rapeseed (canola) oil
2 small round shallots, sliced
60 g (2 oz) lemongrass, finely chopped
40 g (1½ oz) fresh ginger root, finely chopped
2 garlic cloves, roughly chopped
400 g (14 oz) Delica or kabocha pumpkin, peeled, cut into 2.5 cm (1 in) chunks
150 g (5 oz) new potatoes, halved into bite-size pieces
1 heaped tablespoon Vietnamese curry powder or mild curry powder
400 g (14 oz) tin of chickpeas, washed, drained
1 x 225 g (8 oz) tin of bamboo shoot strips (optional)
400 ml (13 fl oz/generous 1½ cups) coconut milk
5 g (¼ oz) palm sugar, roughly chopped
1 teaspoon mushroom seasoning powder or 1 vegetable stock cube
4 lime leaves (optional)
1 tablespoon Yondu vegetable umami sauce, Homemade Vegan Fish Sauce (page 193) or soy sauce
freshly ground black pepper
70 g (2½ oz) sugar snap peas or mangetout (snow peas)
30 g (1 oz) coriander (cilantro) leaves, roughly sliced
zest and juice of 1 lime
20 g (¾ oz) Thai basil (optional)
2 spring onions (scallions), sliced
1 red chilli, sliced (optional)

To serve

a fresh crusty baguette or steamed jasmine rice

Heat the oil in a large saucepan or shallow 30 cm (12 in) casserole dish (Dutch oven) over a medium heat and cook the shallot for about 5 minutes or until golden. Add the lemongrass, ginger and garlic to brown for another 5 minutes before putting in the pumpkin and new potatoes.

Sprinkle over the curry powder and toss everything together so that the pumpkin gets a good coating of the other ingredients. Then throw in the chickpeas and bamboo shoots, if using, and pour over the coconut milk with the sugar, mushroom seasoning and lime leaves, if using. Bring to a gentle simmer over a low heat, cover and cook for 25 minutes. Stirring occasionally.

Season with Yondu vegetable umami sauce and a good pinch of black pepper, and add the sugar snaps. Combine well together in the pan and cook for a further 5 minutes.

Before serving, stir in the coriander and lime zest. Garnish with the Thai basil, if using, and/or more coriander, spring onions and chilli, if using. Squeeze over the fresh lime.

Serve with steamed rice or best with a fresh baguette and butter.

NOTE

If you can't get Delica or kabocha, use butternut squash or any kind of squash/pumpkin. In addition to the vegetables in the ingredients, these can be added or substituted to slices or chunks of courgette (zucchini), cauliflower florets, chunks of marrow, sliced green beans, aubergine (eggplant) asparagus, Tenderstem broccoli, or frozen or fresh garden peas.

# LEMONGRASS VEGETABLE AND PASTA STEW

BÒ KHO CHAY

Warming and comforting yet bursting with zest on colder days and evenings, this is reminiscent of the famous Vietnamese beef stew *bò kho*. It makes good use of winter or summer vegetables and the leftovers are great for breakfast the next day.

Serves 4
Prep time — 20 minutes
Cooking time — 30 minutes

1 tablespoon ghee
2 garlic cloves, finely chopped
60 g (2 oz) lemongrass stalk, finely chopped
½ teaspoon ground turmeric
1 teaspoon ground cumin
1 teaspoon ground coriander (cilantro)
2 celery stalks, cut into 2 cm (¾ in) chunks
110 g (3⅔ oz) carrots, cut into 1 cm (½ in) cubes
50 g (1¾ oz) Jerusalem artichoke, cut into 1 cm (½ in) cubes
100 g (3½ oz) new potatoes, halved
280 g (scant 10 oz) tomatoes, quartered
400 ml (13 fl oz/generous 1½ cups) coconut water
100 g (3½ oz) macaroni or mini pasta shells
3 star anise
2 tablespoons vegetarian oyster sauce
2 tablespoons soy sauce or Homemade Vegan Fish Sauce (page 193)
100 g (3½ oz) savoy cabbage, cut into 1 cm (½ in) strips
300 g (10½ oz) silken tofu
100 g (3½ oz) fresh or frozen garden peas
4 Thai basil sprigs
1 lime, quartered
1 teaspoon chilli (hot pepper) flakes or fresh chillies (optional)

In a wok or frying pan (skillet) over a high heat, add the ghee, garlic and lemongrass, fry for a couple of minutes to release the beautiful aromas, then add the turmeric, cumin and coriander. Fry for a minute, before adding the celery, carrot, Jerusalem artichoke, new potato and tomato. Stir-fry to coat the vegetables in the spices, then add the coconut water, turn the heat down to medium and bring to a gentle boil. Mix in the pasta, star anise, vegetarian oyster sauce and soy sauce. Cover and simmer for 10 minutes, stirring occasionally.

Add the savoy cabbage, mix together to get it wilted, then add the silken tofu and peas. Stir to combine and continue to simmer with the lid on for a further 10 minutes over a medium-low heat, stirring occasionally. If you like the vegetables to have some bite, remove from the heat at this point or simmer for another 5 minutes to soften.

Serve in bowls with steamed jasmine rice or on flat rice noodles. Garnish with the Thai basil, lime wedges and chilli flakes, if using. I also love to have this with a warm French or Vietnamese baguette or toast with a good slather of butter.

NOTE

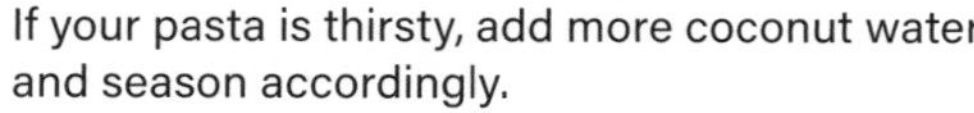

If your pasta is thirsty, add more coconut water and season accordingly.

# VERMICELLI NOODLE SALAD BOWLS

For wonderful summery and memorable meals, you can create noodle bowls using the many toppings dotted throughout this book. Make each bowl beautiful and vibrant with the following must-haves. The more fragrant herbs, the better.

Serves 2

For the salad

2 rice vermicelli nests (0.8 mm) (approx. 160 g (5⅔ oz))
2 big handfuls of anything green and leafy, like lamb's lettuce, watercress, rocket, lettuce and plenty of Vietnamese herbs, washed and dried
2 spring onions (scallions), white and green parts, sliced
2 tablespoons vegetable oil
1 heaped tablespoon peanuts, pistachios or cashews, finely chopped

For the dressing

½ bird's eye chilli, finely chopped
1 tablespoon honey
1 tablespoon perilla sauce, Yondu vegetable umami sauce, soy sauce or Homemade Vegan Fish Sauce (page 193)
finely chopped zest and juice of either ½ lime or ¼ lemon
2 tablespoons hot water
sprig of mint leaves, de-stalked and finely chopped
Quick Pickles (page 204)

For the toppings

Lemongrass Tofu (page 65)
Salt and Pepper Tofu (page 62)
Turmeric and Dill Tofu (page 128)
Sweet and Sour Vegetable Stir-fry (page 58)
Black Bean Aubergines (page 50)
Vegan Vietnamese Sausage (page 117)
Vegetable Spring Rolls (page 118)
Grilled Aubergines with Spring Onion Oil (page 49)
Asparagus Egg Terrine (page 55)

Rehydrate the noodles as directed below.

Place a big handful of salad leaves and herbs into two bowls. Fry the spring onion gently in the oil for 5 minutes, then set aside. Place the noodles to one side of each bowl and smother with the spring onion oil.

To make the salad dressing, place the chilli, honey, perilla sauce, lime zest and juice, hot water and mint into a bowl and mix well together or shake it up in a jar. Decant the dressing in individual serving bowls.

Make the pickle, or use any pickles you already have, such as kimchi or gherkins.

Top with one of the suggested toppings. Garnish with chopped nuts. Pour the dressing over the noodle bowls at the table.

How to rehydrate noodles

Place the noodles in a bowl, pour boiling water over them, cover and leave them to soak for 5–10 minutes. (Different brands vary in cooking times; taste to see if cooked.) Drain, briefly wash with running hot tap water in a sieve or colander, cover and leave to drain off for 10 minutes.

# SIX

# SOUPS FOR THE SOUL

Without phở, I would have trouble existing; I love eating noodle soups for breakfast, lunch, dinner and for midnight snacks. Light, delicate and satisfying Vietnamese noodle soups are on the top of my cravings list.

My daughter Olive was enjoying broth, noodles, greens and leaves even as a toddler. I was so pleased to see her lift her bowl to her face and drink from it. When I was a little girl, my grandmother made sure I did the same. '*Chou Chou, oi,*' she sang and giggled my pet name, cabbage. '*No chưa?*' (Full up yet?).

In the post-war era of Vietnam, my uncle chú Hiển used to set up the Lemongrass Noodle Soup (page 148) breakfast shop for my grandmother every morning at the front of our Sài Gòn home. She was the face and brains of it and he was the brawn that carried the supplies, washed them, sliced them, prepped them, cooked them and so on. My grandmother adjusted the flavours, assembled the bowls and inspected every detail. Afterwards, he would be the one putting it all away before the cycle began again.

A lot of energy goes into making a good broth packed with layers of flavour. The toppings and garnishes bring it all together. It only ever tastes as good as it does because a lot of care and attention to detail goes into making every element work to present the perfect, beautiful bowl of noodle soup. My grandmother would expect every strip of spring onion to be curled, noodles to have the perfect bite and so on. Everything had to be exactly right, my uncle told me.

This synergy was very much the foundation of my supper club which I ran for over a decade with my mum, who made sure everything was as it should be, as she does with every photo in my books. There is no match for a wealth of experience and pure dedication to the food.

And at my supper club, when the broth was done, we would sit down together before service to eat with the friends who helped us along the way. We would take noodles with our chopsticks in one hand, blowing on them to cool and would ladle broth from a spoon into our pursed lips with the other. It was always quiet at first, as we savoured the first mouthfuls, slurping away and only voicing our satisfactions minutes later. My friend Nubi would say, 'This is the best one yet.' Mia: 'How can this be so good? Every. Time!' Aggie would keep slurping the broth, the way she learnt from being my childhood friend, loudly. I would congratulate my mum, '*Ngon quá ngon,*' (very delicious) with the added *ngon* to imply double deliciousness.

# MUSHROOM AND TOFU PHỞ

PHỞ NẤM VÀ ĐẬU HỦ

Many Vietnamese vegetarian meals are simply the vegetarian version of a traditional meat-based dish, created by Buddhist monks. The essential charred onion and ginger, plus the spices, provide the real essence of the much-beloved *phở*, everyone's favourite breakfast.

Serves 6
Prep time — 30 minutes
Cooking time — 1 hour 30 minutes

For the broth

2.5 litres (85 fl oz/10½ cups) approx. water
1.5 kg (3 lb 5 oz) approx. various root vegetables (e.g., carrots, sweet potato, swede, turnip, celeriac, parsnip), peeled, halved or cut into large chunks
2 celery stalks, cut to fit pot
6 dried shiitake mushrooms, rehydrated and sliced
15 g (½ oz) rock sugar
20 g (¾ oz) sea salt
2 vegetable stock cubes or 1 teaspoon MSG
1 onion, peeled, ends trimmed for a flat surface
2 large thumbs of fresh ginger root, peeled and halved lengthways
15 cm (6 in) chunk of daikon, peeled, halved lengthways
1 fennel bulb, halved
10 star anise
1 small Asian cinnamon stick
4 cloves
1 teaspoon coriander seeds
1 teaspoon fennel seeds

For the noodles

75 g (2½ oz) dry flat rice noodles per person
freshly ground black pepper

For the garnish

3 tablespoons vegetable cooking oil
250 g (9 oz) various mushrooms (oyster, fresh shiitake, king, wild), thinly sliced
2 tablespoons vegetarian oyster sauce
120 g (4 oz) block of medium-firm tofu, sliced into 1 cm (½ in) thick rectangles
1 shallot, thinly sliced
15 g (½ oz) coriander (cilantro) leaves, roughly chopped
2 spring onions (scallions), cut into 10 cm (4 in), sliced lengthways into thin strips
1 bird's eye chilli, finely sliced (optional)
3 Thai basil sprigs (optional)
6 soft-boiled eggs (optional)
1 lime, sliced into 6 wedges

Bring a stockpot of the water to a boil with the root vegetables, celery, shiitake, rock sugar, salt and stock cubes.

In a griddle or frying pan (skillet) over a high heat, char the onion, ginger, daikon and fennel on all sides and add to the broth. Turn off the heat. With the residual heat, toast the star anise, cinnamon stick, cloves, coriander seeds and fennel seeds. Feel free to put small ingredients in a piece of muslin (cheesecloth) and add to the broth. Then cover with a lid and cook on a low simmer for 1 hour.

Meanwhile, heat 1 tablespoon of the oil in a medium frying pan (skillet) over a medium heat and fry the mushrooms with the vegetarian oyster sauce for about 5 minutes, or until they have wilted. Set aside.

In the same pan, fry the tofu in the rest of the oil for 8 minutes on each side until golden and drain on paper towels. Set aside.

Rehydrate the noodles by placing them in a bowl by pouring just-boiled water from the kettle over them. Cover for at least 4 minutes or until cooked. When done, drain in a colander and rinse with hot tap water until it runs clear of starch. Then place a lid on the colander to dry out and fluff up.

Using a spider, remove all the vegetables and spices from the broth and slice any vegetables that you wish to eat. Discard the onion, ginger, celery or anything that has gone too mushy.

Portion the noodles into noodle bowls and season with a pinch of black pepper. Place the tofu, fried mushrooms and sliced vegetables on top of the noodles, before adding the shallot, coriander, spring onion, chilli and Thai basil, if using. If using, then place the eggs into each bowl, slicing them at the last minute into halves. Bring the pot of broth back to the boil.

When ready to serve, ladle over the boiling hot broth, making sure that everything is submerged. Serve immediately. Add a good squeeze of lime juice at the table.

# BÁNH CANH NOODLE SOUP

BÁNH CANH CHAY

Some of the best *bánh canh* (literally means 'soup noodles') can be found in my mum's hometown Phan Thiết, from street stalls run by ladies with years of experience of making and selling just this one dish. In fact, the whole culinary experience in Phan Thiết is phenomenal and I recommend you visit. This amazingly quick, easy and delicious dish is a winner on all days of the year. The flavour of the broth is enhanced by crispy fried shallot oil and lots of fresh lime. You can use any greens and toppings to make this as simple or intricate as you like. I highly recommend spending 20 minutes making the fresh-cut bánh canh noodles. You can even cook the noodles in the broth, making it slightly thicker and comforting.

Serves 2
Prep time — approx. 30 minutes
Cooking time — approx. 30 minutes

- 2 x 200 g (7 oz) bundles of Homemade Bánh Canh Noodles (page 198) or 2 x 200 g (7 oz) packets of fresh udon noodles
- 1 litre (34 fl oz/4 cups) boiling water or Homemade Vegetable Stock (page 196)
- 2 tablespoons nutritional yeast or 1 teaspoon mushroom seasoning powder
- 1 vegetable stock cube (if using water instead of homemade stock)
- 1 tablespoon Homemade Vegan Fish Sauce (page 193) or Yondu vegetable umami sauce
- 2 tablespoons vegetable oil
- 2 shallots, sliced into half-moons
- 20 g (¾ oz) dill or coriander (cilantro) leaves, roughly chopped
- freshly ground black pepper
- 200 g (7 oz) greens, such as pak choi (bok choi), Chinese broccoli leaves, mustard leaves, watercress or spinach
- 2 large lime wedges

Additional topping options

- Vegan Vietnamese Sausage, sliced into 5 mm (¼ in) width discs (page 117) (optional)
- Sweet Potato and Water Chestnut Wontons (page 27)
- Pan-fried Vegetable Dumplings (page 21 or 22)
- Asparagus Egg Terrine (page 55)

Follow the instructions to make homemade bánh canh noodles. If using udon, rehydrate them in a saucepan with boiling water from the kettle, let them sit for 5 minutes then drain and portion into noodle soup bowls.

Pour the water into a saucepan, add the nutritional yeast, stock cube (if required) and vegan fish sauce and simmer over a medium heat with the lid on.

In a separate frying pan (skillet), add the oil and shallot and let it sit on a medium-low heat for about 5 minutes, giving it an occasional stir until they start to turn golden. Divide between the two bowls, pouring the remaining oil into the broth.

Garnish the bowls with dill or coriander (or both), black pepper, additional toppings as you desire and your choice of greens. (If using pak choi, Chinese broccoli leaves or mustard leaves, you need to blanch these first.)

Bring the broth to a boil and ladle over the noodles. Serve immediately with lime wedges.

# SOUTHERN NOODLE SOUP

HỦ TIẾU CHAY

The north of Vietnam has phở. *Hủ tiếu* is the Southern speciality. The complex layers of broth are boosted by fried garlic and garlic oil, lots of garlic chives and celery leaves. It is fascinating how small steps make a huge difference to the overall taste. The toppings can be as simple or as elaborate as you like. To make this the perfect Sài Gòn experience, enjoy this wonderful noodle soup with Vietnamese Dough Sticks to dunk in the broth (page 32).

Serves 4
Prep time — 45 minutes
Cooking time — 1 hour

For the broth

2 litres (70 fl oz/8 cups) water or Homemade Vegetable Stock (page 196)
1 onion, charred
20 g (¾ oz) fresh ginger root, peeled
1 Asian pear, peeled, core removed, halved
1 red apple, core removed, quartered
15 cm (6 in) daikon, peeled
1 carrot
1 celery stalk

For the broth seasoning

20 g (¾ oz) rock sugar
25 g (¾ oz) sea salt
2 teaspoons nutritional yeast
1 teaspoon sesame oil
2 tablespoons rapeseed (canola) oil
4 large garlic cloves, finely chopped

For the toppings

1½ tablespoons rapeseed (canola) oil
200 g (7 oz) medium-firm tofu, cut into batons and fried for 8 minutes on both sides, or tofu puffs
100 g (3½ oz) various fresh mushrooms
1 tablespoon vegetarian oyster sauce
200 g (7 oz) Tenderstem broccoli
12 quail's eggs
handful of bean sprouts
2 tablespoons Crispy Shallots (page 208)

For the noodles

Hủ tiếu noodles (flat thin tapioca noodles), rice noodles or ramen noodles

For the garnish

40 g (1½ oz) garlic chives, snipped into 4 cm (1½ in) pieces
celery leaves, rough torn
freshly ground black pepper
1 bird's eye chilli, sliced (optional)
1 lime, quartered

Additional toppings

wontons (page 27), dumplings (page 21 or 22), Vegan Vietnamese Sausage (page 117)

Bring the water to a boil in a large saucepan and simmer for about 45 minutes with the charred onion, ginger, Asian pear, apple, daikon, carrot and celery. Season with the rock sugar, sea salt and nutritional yeast. Add the sesame oil after 45 minutes and turn off the heat.

In a frying pan (skillet) over a medium heat, add the rapeseed oil and fry the garlic. Watch until it turns golden and immediately decant the oil and garlic from the pan into a heatproof bowl.

For the toppings, add 1 tablespoon of the oil to the same pan and over a medium heat, fry the tofu and mushrooms together with the vegetarian oyster sauce and 1 tablespoon of the crispy shallots. When the mushrooms have softened, set aside and add the remaining rapeseed oil to the same pan and fry the broccoli.

Boil the quail's eggs for 4 minutes, peel them, then cut into halves. Bring a full kettle to the boil, place the bean sprouts into a bowl and blanch them for 2 minutes. Use the rest of the boiling water to rehydrate the noodles (page 137).

Assemble your bowls with the Hủ tiếu noodles, bean sprouts, the tofu, mushrooms, broccoli, quail's eggs, fried garlic, crispy shallots, garlic chives and celery leaves. Add any of the vegetables you desire from the broth. I love thinly sliced daikon in this and additional toppings such as wontons.

To serve, bring the broth to a boil and ladle over the noodles. Serve with black pepper, sliced chillies (if using) and the lime wedges.



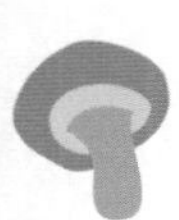

# LEMONGRASS NOODLE SOUP

BÚN BÒ HUẾ CHAY

It is crucial to dedicate time and love to the broth. Choose as many toppings as you like, and endeavour to perfect and make everything look as beautiful as it tastes. This is how my mother, her mother and those before her showed their love and affection: through the eyes into the belly.

Serves 6

Prep time — 30 minutes–1 hour 30 minutes

Cooking time — at least 1 hour 30 minutes

For the broth

40 g (1½ oz) dried shiitake or wild mushrooms
3 litres Homemade Vegetable Stock, including the vegetables (page 196)
1 large onion, charred
2 lime leaves
2 teaspoons sea salt
20 g (¾ oz) palm or rock sugar
2 tablespoons nutritional yeast
3 tablespoons Homemade Vegan Fish Sauce (page 193)
3 lemongrass stalks
3–4 tablespoons vegetable oil
300 g (10½ oz) medium-firm tofu, sliced into batons

For the lemongrass and chilli paste

100 ml (3½ fl oz/scant ½ cup) vegetable oil
10 g (⅓ oz) annatto seeds
3 tablespoons Lemongrass and Chilli Oil (page 210)

For the noodles

thick rice vermicelli (1.2–1.8 mm)

For the toppings

3–4 tablespoons vegetable oil
200 g (7 oz) tofu puffs, halved
100 g (3½ oz) enoki or various mushrooms, sliced
1 tablespoon vegetarian oyster sauce
leafy greens, such as water spinach, choi sum, pak choi (bok choi), blanched, or courgette (zucchini) flowers

For the toppings (optional)

Lemongrass Tofu (page 65)
Vegan Vietnamese Sausage (page 117)

For the garnish (optional)

Thai basil, bean sprouts, coriander (cilantro) leaves, curled spring onions (scallions), Vietnamese coriander
1 lime, quartered
1 bird's eye chilli, sliced

Rehydrate the dried mushrooms in a bowl with 150 ml (5 fl oz/scant ⅔ cup) of just-boiled water – do not discard the water.

Add the vegetable stock, onion, lime leaves, salt and sugar to a stockpot. Bring to a simmering boil then cook for 30 minutes with the lid on. Season with nutritional yeast and vegan fish sauce. Bash the lemongrass with the back of a knife or rolling pin and place it over a gas flame to char or in a dry frying pan (skillet) until its sides are blackened. Add the lemongrass to the stockpot plus the mushrooms and their soaking water and simmer for another 30 minutes.

While the broth is simmering, make the lemongrass and chilli paste. Add the oil to a frying pan over a medium heat with the annatto seeds. The red colour of the seeds should release into the oil. Stir and cook for a few minutes. Using a small strainer or sieve, strain the red oil into a small bowl and discard the seeds. Mix together with the lemongrass and chilli oil.

Divide the paste into two. Add one half to the broth and use the other half to marinate the tofu puffs for 30 minutes.

In the same pan over a medium heat, add a tablespoon of the oil and fry the tofu for 3 minutes, then add the mushrooms and vegetarian oyster sauce. Fry until they have softened and work through a handful of the leafy greens for 1–2 minutes. Set aside.

Cook the noodles in a pot of boiling water for 10 minutes or until al dente, stirring occasionally to prevent them from sticking to the bottom. Drain in a colander and run under warm water until the starch runs clear. Place a lid over the noodles to dry them out for at least 10 minutes.

When the broth has finished cooking, use a spider to remove the vegetables. Slice the (dried) mushrooms and any other vegetables you desire as toppings into bite-size pieces.

Assemble soup bowls with the noodles and any vegetables, mushrooms, green leaves, tofu puffs, any additional toppings you would like and garnishes as desired.

Bring the broth to a boil and ladle it into the assembled bowls. Serve with a squeeze of lime and sliced chillies, if desired.

# EGG AND TOMATO NOODLE SOUP

BÚN RIÊU CHAY

Usually served as a light lunch or supper, this is the way to go. It is sometimes served after a very big feast when, a few hours later, our bellies start to rumble again and we need to warm up. This can be simple or elaborate, depending on your garnishes. The silky eggs are gorgeous in the tomato-based broth.

Serves 2
Prep time — 20 minutes
Cooking time — 30 minutes

For the broth

850 ml (scant 29 fl oz/generous 3½ cups) just-boiled water or Homemade Vegetable Stock (page 196)
4 g (⅛ oz) dried wild mushrooms, washed
1 tablespoon vegetable bouillon, vegetable stock cube or 1 teaspoon mushroom seasoning powder
1 lemongrass stalk, bashed with back of a knife
1 tablespoon cooking oil
1 shallot, sliced
3 garlic cloves, sliced
120 g (4 oz) cherry tomatoes, halved
1 tablespoon tomato purée (paste)
pinch of sea salt
10 g (⅓ oz) rock sugar or 1 teaspoon sugar
3 eggs, beaten
1 spring onion (scallion)
1 teaspoon Homemade Vegan Fish Sauce (page 193), plus 1 tablespoon
juice of 2 limes

For the noodles

50 g (1¾ oz) rice vermicelli (0.8 mm) per person
½ portion of Lemongrass Tofu (page 65) or plain, fried tofu (page 61)

For the garnish (optional)

coriander (cilantro) leaves
mint
1 spring onion (scallion), sliced lengthways, soaked in cold water
Thai basil
freshly ground black pepper
Thai parsley or sawtooth
banana blossom, shredded
water spinach stems (morning glory), shredded
2 lime wedges
bird's eye chillies

Pour the water or stock into a large saucepan. Turn the heat on to the lowest setting and add the mushrooms, vegetable bouillon and lemongrass. Simmer gently for 10 minutes to soften the mushrooms and infuse the lemongrass into the liquid.

In a frying pan (skillet) or wok, add the oil and gently fry the shallot and garlic over a medium heat until they turn golden. Then add the tomatoes and tomato purée and cook for 2–3 minutes with the salt and sugar. Add the entire contents to the broth.

Place the noodles in a container and pour just-boiled water over them. Cover for 10 minutes then drain, rinse well with hot water and leave in a colander, covered, for 10 minutes.

Assemble two bowls with the noodles, tofu and any garnishes you like.

In a measuring jug, whisk the eggs with the spring onion and 1 teaspoon of the vegan fish sauce.

Bring the pan of broth to a boil over a high heat. Using a long-handled spoon, stir the broth in a circular motion and gently pour in the egg mix, so the eggs cook in the whirling broth and fluff up into clouds.

Add the cooked eggs and tomatoes to the noodle bowls. To the broth, add half of the lime juice and 1 tablespoon of the vegan fish sauce and bring to a boil. Then ladle the hot broth over the bowls.

Serve immediately with the lime wedges and desired garnishes.

# QUICK MUSHROOM NOODLE SOUP



MÌ NẤM

So much flavour is extracted when rehydrating dried mushrooms and this is fantastic for making a quick broth and enjoying with lots of greens.

Serves 1
Prep time — 15 minutes
Cooking time — 25 minutes
Soaking time — 20 minutes

10 g (⅓ oz) dried mushrooms
125 ml (generous 4 fl oz/generous ½ cup) just-boiled water
60 g (2 oz) ramen, flat rice noodles or soba
70 g (2½ oz) leafy greens, such as Chinese broccoli, pak choi (bok choi), watercress, Chinese cabbage, mustard leaves
300 ml (10 fl oz/1¼ cups) just-boiled water or Homemade Vegetable Stock (page 196)
1 tablespoon light soy sauce
1 tablespoon dark soy sauce
1 tablespoon nutritional yeast or ½ vegetable stock cube
1 egg, boiled to your liking
1 spring onion (scallion), thinly sliced
1 teaspoon sesame oil (optional)

Rehydrate the mushrooms with the just-boiled water in a bowl for 15–20 minutes. De-stalk and slice the mushrooms thinly. Retain the soaking water.

Cook the noodles as per packet instructions.

Place the greens in a bowl, blanch with just-boiled water for 5 minutes and drain.

Add the water or stock to a saucepan with the mushroom soaking water, both soy sauces and the nutritional yeast. Simmer for 5 minutes.

Assemble your bowl with the noodles, mushrooms and greens. Bring the broth to a full boil, ladle the broth into the bowl, then quickly add the egg, halved, and the spring onion. Top with sesame oil, if using, and any other condiments you like.



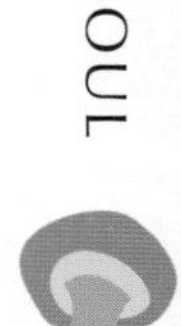

# SWEET AND SOUR TOMATO AND GOLDEN BEETROOT SOUP

CANH CHUA CHAY

This vibrant soup will bring sunshine to the table. Tomatoes are always a must, but they can also be paired with pineapple, taro root, rice paddy herb and bean sprouts. This is a quick 'cook', as the vegetables must retain their form and bite, so have everything ready by the stove. Taste throughout, as the magic comes from the balance of flavours. As the ingredients here will vary in sweetness and sharpness, add only half of the seasonings first and more as required, but remember it is meant to be both sweet and sour.

Serves 4
Prep time — 15 minutes
Cooking time — 12 minutes

750 ml (25 fl oz/3 cups) water or unseasoned Homemade Vegetable Stock (page 196)
1½ vegetable stock cubes
1 tablespoon rapeseed (canola) oil
4 garlic cloves, finely chopped
2 tablespoons Homemade Vegan Fish Sauce (page 193)
100 g (3½ oz) golden beetroot (beets), peeled, sliced into bite-size quarters
2 tomatoes, cut into eighths
2½ tablespoons coconut sugar or 1½ tablespoons caster (superfine) sugar
2 (25 cm (10 in) each) rhubarb sticks
50 g (1¾ oz) bean sprouts (optional)
20 g (¾ oz) dill, snipped into 4 cm (1½ in) lengths
1 bird's eye chilli, sliced at a diagonal
juice of 1 lime

For the garnish (optional)

tofu
Vegan Vietnamese Sausages (page 117)
sliced omelette

Bring the water to a boil in a saucepan with the stock cubes.

Meanwhile, in a small saucepan over a low heat, add the oil and cook the garlic until it turns golden, then immediately transfer into a small bowl and set aside.

When the broth comes to the boil, turn the heat down to medium, add the vegan fish sauce, beetroot, tomatoes and sugar. Simmer for 5 minutes then add the rhubarb and simmer for another 5 minutes. Then add the bean sprouts, if using, and dill. Turn off the heat and pour into a large serving soup bowl. Snip in the bird's eye chilli, add the fried garlic and give it a stir and a good squeeze of lime.

Serve as a sharing bowl with rice and other dishes or ladle over a bowl of vermicelli noodles, topped with tofu, vegan sausages or sliced omelette. You could also serve the soup in individual bowls.

NOTE

If rhubarb is not in season, use tinned or fresh pineapple, celery or taro root. If you can't get golden beetroot (beets), use chayotes, kohlrabi, daikon or Asian pear.

# WATERCRESS, GINGER AND SILKEN TOFU SOUP

CANH CẢI XÀ LÁCH XOONG

Easy, quick and refreshing, serve this soup as a warming palate-cleanser between mouthfuls of rice.

Makes 4 small bowls
Prep time — 5 minutes
Cooking time — 5 minutes

700 ml (24 fl oz/scant 3 cups) water
20 g (¾ oz) fresh ginger root, peeled, thinly sliced
2 tablespoons nutritional yeast or 1 teaspoon mushroom bouillon
1 teaspoon sea salt
150 g (5 oz) silken tofu, cut into 1 cm (½ in) cubes
100 g (3½ oz) watercress, snipped into 10 cm (4 in) lengths

Bring the water to a boil in a saucepan, then add the ginger, nutritional yeast and salt. Add the tofu then bring back to a boil. Add the watercress and cook for 2 minutes. Done!

# ANY VEG RICE PORRIDGE

CHÁO

*Cháo* (rice porridges) are a great canvas for seasonal vegetables. Simply simmer rice and water or broth together until the grains have bloomed. Eaten for breakfast or when you're unwell, the healing component of ginger is especially comforting. This recipe uses uncooked rice, but if you have leftover cooked rice add it to the broth and simmer for less time, although brown or wild rice will take longer to cook. As a cook, I particularly love to add, taste and further create. Raid the refrigerator. Open the larder door. There is no right or wrong, but cook harder vegetables a little longer and softer ones towards the end. Carrot and coriander (cilantro); pumpkin and ginger; turmeric and asparagus; marrow and Jerusalem artichoke; winter melon and watercress; carrot, peas and courgette (zucchini); radicchio, courgette and broad beans; red beans and chilli oil, cabbage and dill – the possibilities are endless. You can also top your porridge with any leftovers such as Spiced Tofu with Aubergine and Enoki Mushrooms (page 66), Lemongrass Tofu (page 65), Water Spinach with Capers (page 43).

Serves 4
Prep time — 5–15 minutes
Cooking time — 35 minutes

750 ml (25 fl oz/3 cups) water or Homemade Vegetable Stock (page 196)
½ tablespoon sea salt
5 g (¼ oz) rock sugar
½ teaspoon mushroom bouillon or stock cube (if using water)
125 g (4 oz/scant ⅔ cup) jasmine rice, rinsed three times, drained
20 g (¾ oz) fresh ginger root, peeled, finely chopped
500 g (1 lb 2 oz) any vegetables you like
1 tablespoon Yondu vegetable umami sauce, pinch of salt or Homemade Vegan Fish Sauce (page 193)
¼ teaspoon freshly ground black pepper

For the garnish

spring onions (scallions), sliced
any herb like coriander (cilantro) leaves, basil, garlic chives, celery leaves, roughly torn
Crispy Shallots (page 208)
freshly ground black pepper
bird's eye chillies, sliced (optional)

Pour the just-boiled water into a saucepan and season with salt, sugar and mushroom bouillon.

Add the rice to the broth with the ginger. Cover the pan and bring to a boil, then turn down to low, skimming off any foam and stirring occasionally to stop the bottom from catching. Continue to simmer for about 10 minutes then add any hard vegetables. Cook for a further 10 minutes still over a low heat, then add any soft vegetables. By this stage, the rice grains should be blossoming and the broth thickened. Season with the vegetable umami sauce and cook for 5 more minutes.

To serve, heat the porridge gently, then ladle into individual soup bowls and scatter with garnishes.

NOTE

You can play with the texture of the porridge by cooking for more or less time, and adding more or less liquid. It is up to you!

# SEVEN

# SWEET TREATS

Eating for pleasure is paramount; in Vietnamese, mouths must literally be sweetened (*ngọt miệng*). This means sweet things are as equally important as main meals.

As it is not traditional to cook in ovens, my mum didn't know how to make cakes. So, whenever I was allowed in the kitchen, this was what I did, all by trial and error as we didn't have any cookbooks or recipes. My mum loves patisserie – another French influence that took a stronghold in Vietnamese culture – and she is a discerning judge. As a teenager, I spent my weekends mastering the perfect sponge cake which is very popular in Vietnam.

Sweet things often remind me of my mum's fellow refugee friend who was also our babysitter. A four-foot, five-inch Cambodian lady called bác Liên (now well into her 90s), she had a very coarse, loud, animated voice. She was always perfectly dressed, with self-made knitwear and beautifully blow-dried 50s-style hair.

When pandan became available, it was big news, and I remember my mum and her joyously splitting the fragrant leaves between them into the crackly plastic grocery bags, counting out coins to pay while giving each other careful preserving and cooking instructions. They counselled each other on its health benefits, steamed plenty of cakes and added the extract to sweet, soupy desserts.

Bác Liên always came with a bamboo basket of pandan-infused goods every weekend. In exchange, she asked for me and my brother to teach her English. This went on for years, as her flawlessly coiffed hair grew whiter. She brought rice-flour honeycomb cake (which I have yet to master), mung bean layer cake and chiffon sponge cake. And she would only ever remember: 'How are you?', 'I would like to buy fish', 'Thank you very much' and 'More, please', but it was enough for her to get by.

# PANDAN BAKED BURNT BASQUE CHEESECAKE

BÁNH BÔNG LAN PHÔ MAI

I love an easy dessert, especially because I like to make plenty of savoury dishes whenever I cook. You can get this cake done and dusted, chilling in the refrigerator early on, while everything else is still on the go. Its texture is softer than the traditional Basque cake and the pandan gives it a soothing kiss; pandan leaves are the secret to all exquisiteness. As you peel off the burnt paper at the table, prepare for your guests to fight for a slice.

Serves 8
Prep time — 15 minutes
Cooking time — 1 hour
Chilling time — 2–6 hours

½ tablespoon cooking spray or vegetable oil
100 g (3½ oz) fresh pandan leaves, cut into 5 cm (2 in) strips, washed
150 ml (5 fl oz/scant ⅔ cup) coconut water or water
800 g (1 lb 12 oz) cream cheese, room temperature
190 g (6¾ oz) caster (superfine) sugar
4 eggs
2 tablespoons plain (all-purpose) flour
200 ml (7 fl oz/scant 1 cup) coconut milk or double (heavy) cream
¼ teaspoon sea salt

Preheat a fan oven to 220°C (425°F/gas 7) and place the oven rack on the middle shelf.

Grease a deep 20 cm (8 in) loose-bottom or springform cake tin (pan) with the cooking spray or oil and line it with two large sheets of baking parchment (approximately 40 cm (15¾ in) length), one twisted at 45 degrees on top of the other, with the corners pointing in different directions like a star. Crumple the parchment into the tin, pressing into the corners, and roughly crease up and pleat the sides to fit the tin, but making sure plenty of paper is still sticking out above the rim.

To make the pandan extract, add the leaves to a blender with the coconut water and blend to a pulp. Pour everything over a sieve into a bowl and squeeze out the extract with your hands. (You can reuse the leaves for a second extraction for another recipe before discarding the pulp.)

Add the cream cheese to a large free-standing mixer bowl. Beat with a paddle attachment on medium-low speed for about 3 minutes or with an electric whisk, gradually adding the sugar until the grains have dissolved. Scrape everything back down into the bowl. Continue to mix, adding one egg at a time until everything is fully incorporated and thickened.

Sieve the flour into the bowl, add the coconut milk, pandan extract and salt and mix again until it is smooth. The mixture should be quite runny. Pour it into the lined cake tin, place the tin on a baking tray (pan) and then bake for 25 minutes. You will see that the top is looking burnt, but this is how it is meant to look. At this point, I like to place a piece of kitchen foil or baking parchment on top to prevent it from blackening. Bake for a further 35 minutes.

Once cooked, the cheesecake should be domed and puffy like a soufflé. It might also be cracked (this is okay) and it will still be wobbly when you shake the tin. Leave it to cool completely in the tin – it will sink as it cools. Then chill for at least 2 hours before serving, although it is best to leave it for 5–6 hours. It will keep in the fridge for up to 2 days.

# VIETNAMESE COFFEE ICE CREAM

KEM CÀ PHÊ

When it's too hot for a cup of coffee, but you still crave a fix, it's hard to resist the famous Vietnamese iced coffee known as *cà phê sữa đá* and this is a delicious take on that drink that will end a feast perfectly on a sultry summer's day. To make any coffee fiend weak at the knees, I love to brew extra black Vietnamese coffee in a Vietnamese coffee maker (*phin*) and then pour it over scoops of the ice cream like an Italian *affogato*.

Serves 6–8
Prep time — 10 minutes
Churning time — 1 hour–1 hour 10 minutes
Chilling time — 4 hours or overnight

3 sachets of instant Vietnamese coffee
or 3 tablespoons ground Vietnamese coffee
300 ml (10 fl oz/1¼ cups) just-boiled water
300 g (10½ oz) condensed milk
300 ml (10 fl oz/1¼ cups) double (heavy) cream

If using instant Vietnamese coffee, empty the sachets into a bowl or saucepan with the just-boiled water and condensed milk and stir well.

If using ground coffee, make three separate cups of coffee using the just-boiled water in a Vietnamese coffee maker. Then add these coffees to a bowl or saucepan with the condensed milk and stir well.

Add the cream to the coffee mixture in the bowl and combine together. Pour the mixture into an ice-cream machine and churn for 1 hour–1 hour 10 minutes. Transfer the mixture to a freezer-safe container and freeze for at least 4 hours or overnight.

If you do not have an ice-cream machine, transfer the mixture to a freezer-safe container and place it in the freezer. After 2 hours, use a fork to mash the mixture well and evenly. Repeat after 4 hours and then freeze for a further 2 hours.

# BANANA, COCONUT AND TAPIOCA PUDDING

CHÈ CHUỐI

Usually, the popular sweet soupy dessert known as *chè* (sometimes compared to bubble tea) is eaten in the evenings or as a cooling snack during the day. This is a soothing, sweet and warm dessert for all coconut and banana lovers and it's really easy to make. If you can get hold of small Asian finger bananas, they will draw out the true flavour of this dessert, but it's fine to use the standard Cavendish type as set out below.

Serves 4–6
Prep time — 5 minutes
Cooking time — 15–20 minutes

500 ml (17 fl oz/2 cups) coconut water or water
35 g (1¼ oz) palm sugar
100 g (3½ oz) small white tapioca pearls
200 ml (7 fl oz/scant 1 cup) coconut milk
4 just-ripe finger bananas or 2 just-ripe standard bananas, sliced, 5 mm (¼ in) on the diagonal
1 tablespoon roasted, salted peanuts, chopped or crushed

In a saucepan over a medium heat, bring the coconut water and sugar to a gentle boil, then add the tapioca pearls. Simmer for 5 minutes and stir occasionally to prevent it from catching at the bottom. Add the coconut milk and banana and simmer for another 5 minutes. Remove from the heat and serve warm (or chilled) in little bowls, garnished with the chopped peanuts.

NOTE

Instead of banana, you can use pumpkin, taro, sweet potato or sweetcorn. If you make this ahead, the tapioca balls will continue to absorb coconut milk, expand and cling to each other, so break up any clumps with a fork, adding coconut water to loosen.



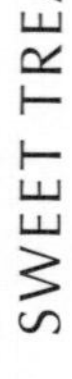

# LOTUS AND PURPLE SWEET POTATO RICE PUDDING



CHÈ KHOAI LANG CỦ SEN

The lilac tint to this special rice pudding comes from succulent purple sweet potato which is embraced by the soft, sweet coconut rice, contrasting with the beautiful, crunchy geometric rounds of lotus root. This dish is also full of goodness as the ingredients are noted for their nutritional and medicinal benefits.

Serves 4–6
Prep time — 10 minutes
Soaking time — 30 minutes
Cooking time — 25 minutes

200 g (7 oz) glutinous rice, soaked at least 30 minutes or overnight, drained
700 ml (24 fl oz/scant 3 cups) coconut water
60 g (2 oz) palm sugar
250 g (9 oz) purple sweet potato, peeled and cut into 2 cm (¾ in) cubes
170 g (scant 6 oz) lotus root, peeled and sliced into 5 mm (¼ in) discs (halve any that seem too big)
150 g (5 oz) tinned lotus seeds (drained weight)
400 ml (13 fl oz/generous 1½ cups) coconut milk

In a saucepan over a medium heat, add the rice, 400 ml (13 fl oz/generous 1½ cups) of the coconut water, the palm sugar, sweet potato and lotus root. Mix together, cover and bring to a boil, then turn down to the lowest heat. Stir occasionally for 15 minutes and make sure the bottom does not catch and burn. Add a little of the remaining coconut water as it thickens and keep adding more every time you stir. Then add the lotus seeds with 150 ml (5 fl oz/scant ⅔ cup) of the coconut milk, folding through the rice, and cook for a further 5–10 minutes.

Serve warm, topped with the rest of the coconut milk.

NOTES

Substitutions: sweet potato, black-eyed peas, red kidney beans, adzuki beans.

If you can't get fresh lotus root, try sliced tinned water chestnuts.

# FRUITY TRIFLE

BÁNH TRÁI CÂY NHIỀU TẦNG

When we were growing up, my mum would often buy us supermarket trifles as a treat. Like many things that I hold close to my heart, like queuing in line and having a good cup of builder's tea, trifle is up there on my Britishness list. I love making a showstopper trifle on special occasions such as Christmases, birthdays or if someone is visiting. Nicely decorated desserts always seem to make everyone really happy, so they get more and more elaborate every time. The best thing is I often use shop-bought ingredients because I would have spent a lot of time cooking the rest of the meal and need a stress-free dessert. Use as many fruits as you like or just one or two kinds of fruit. I use ginger beer here, but feel free to use any other juice such as coconut water or aloe vera.

Serves 6–8
Prep time — at least 1 hour
Cooking time — 10 minutes–2 hours
Soaking/setting time — at least 40 minutes

For the jelly layer

1½ level teaspoons agar flakes
450 ml (15¼ fl oz/scant 2 cups) ginger beer
2 tablespoons caster (superfine) sugar
5 strawberries
handful of raspberries, halved
dragon fruit, cubed
1 kiwi, peeled, halved, finely sliced

For the cake layer

½ Pandan and Coconut 'Birthday' Cake (page 174) or shop-bought trifle sponge fingers
200 ml (7 fl oz/scant 1 cup) Malibu or Cointreau (optional)

For the custard layer

600 ml (20 fl oz/2½ cups) shop-bought custard

For the cream layer

300 ml (10 fl oz/1¼ cups) double (heavy) cream
1 tablespoon icing (confectioner's) sugar

For the toppings (optional)

Suggestions: meringue kisses, tinned peaches, sliced strawberries, chocolate flakes, jackfruit, dragon fruit, lychees, kiwi

Soak the agar flakes in the ginger beer and sugar for 30 minutes in a saucepan. Then turn on a low heat and gently bring to a simmer. Refrain from stirring and wait until it is just hot but not boiling. Stir gently for 5 minutes until the agar flakes have dissolved, making sure it does not reach a boil. Let it cool to room temperature.

Meanwhile, place the fruit for your jelly in the trifle bowl or glasses.

When the agar mixture has cooled, pour it onto the fruit and let it set in the refrigerator for 10–30 minutes or until set.

When the jelly has set, layer the pandan cake on top and drizzle Malibu all over, if using. Then pour over the custard on top of the cake.

When ready to serve, whisk the cream together with the icing sugar. When it forms soft peaks, layer it on top of the custard. Decorate with your chosen toppings.

# PANDAN 'BIRTHDAY' CAKE

BÁNH BÔNG LAN LÁ DỨA

'Why can't we have birthday cake?' my brother complains, 'I want birthday cake!' 'But it isn't anyone's birthday!' I'd say. 'I know', he'd reply, 'but I still want birthday cake'. Light and fluffy sponge cakes are well-loved and much-craved in Vietnamese culture. Birthday cakes are usually decorated with clouds of squirty cream, floral piping and the works, including the birthday boy's or girl's name in fancy script, so feel free to go to town. Or keep it understated and simply indulge in its soft, spongey and delicate texture with a soothing cup of tea.

Makes 1 cake
Prep time — 25 minutes
Cooking time — 55 minutes

For the pandan extract

50 g (1¾ oz) fresh pandan leaves, cut into 5 cm (2 in) strips, washed
70 ml (2½ oz/⅓ cups) water

For the dry ingredients

100 g (3½ oz) self-raising flour
¼ teaspoon salt
1½ teaspoons baking powder
1 tablespoon coconut or vegetable oil, for greasing

For the wet ingredients

5 large egg yolks, room temperature
60 ml (2 fl oz/¼ cup) coconut oil (or neutral oil)
60 ml (2 fl oz/¼ cup) coconut milk, room temperature (or milk)

For the meringue

5 egg whites, room temperature
140 g (scant 5 oz) caster (superfine) sugar

Place the rack in the middle of a fan oven and preheat to 200°C (400°F/gas 6). Line a fixed-base 20 cm (8 in) cake tin (pan) with baking parchment.

To make the pandan extract, add the leaves to a blender with the water and blend to a pulp. Pour everything over a sieve into a bowl and squeeze out the extract with your hands.

Sieve the flour, salt and baking powder into a large bowl, then combine with the egg yolks, coconut oil, coconut milk and pandan extract. Mix together with a spatula until smooth and set aside.

In a squeaky-clean free-standing mixer (or bowl if using an electric whisk), whip up the egg whites. When the whites have formed soft peaks, gently and slowly sprinkle the sugar into the meringue. Continue to whisk for about 5 minutes on a medium-high speed until it has formed stiffer peaks.

Using a clean spatula, mix a quarter of the meringue into the bowl of wet ingredients. When that has combined, gently fold in another quarter until that has combined and repeat.

Pour into the cake tin and place in a bain-marie (with boiling water from the kettle), turn down the oven to 160°C (320°F/gas 2) and bake for 55–60 minutes.

Do not open the oven during this time. The cake should form a dome and brown on top. To check if the cake has cooked through, poke in a metal skewer, which should come out clean if it is cooked. If not, continue to bake for another 5–10 minutes until it slides out clean. When done, rest for at least 10 minutes then remove the cake from the tin by lifting the paper out and leave to cool on a rack.

Slice the cake in half horizontally if you would like to add a layer of cream and then decorate to your heart's desire.

NOTE

Use leftover sponge cake for a refreshing Fruity Trifle (page 172).

# RAINBOW DESSERT

CHÈ SƯƠNG SA HẠT LỰU

The name of this dessert translates as jelly and pomegranate (*hạt lựu*) but the 'pomegranate' is actually water chestnut, so not only are the Vietnamese masters at making cooling and refreshing desserts, they are also extremely creative. This is my all-time favourite and the dessert of my childhood dreams. My mum only ever made it when I had playdates with my best friend Agnieszka. We would sit in science class years later, thinking about sinking a long dessert spoon down into the sweet bean paste at the bottom and dragging it to the top with the crunchy faux pomegranates and refreshing jelly. To this day, we still dream.

Serves 4
Prep time — 40 minutes
Cooking time — 35–40 minutes

For the agar jelly

- 500 ml (17 fl oz/2 cups) coconut water
- ¾ teaspoon shop-bought pandan extract
- 1½ teaspoons agar flakes
- 1½ tablespoons caster (superfine) sugar

For the sweet bean paste

- 100 g (3½ oz) split mung beans, soaked 30 minutes (150 g (5 oz) when cooked)
- 60 ml (2 fl oz/¼ cup) coconut milk
- 3 tablespoons agave syrup or maple syrup

For the 'pomegranates'

- 200 g (7 oz) water chestnuts, cut into 5 mm (¼ in) cubes
- 1 tablespoon beetroot (beet) juice or ½ teaspoon pink or red food colouring
- 50 g (1¾ oz) tapioca starch

For the coconut

- 1 whole young coconut (optional) or 300 ml (10 fl oz) coconut water
- 200 ml (7 fl oz/scant 1 cup) coconut milk
- 3 pandan leaves, knotted
- 16 g (generous ½ oz) palm sugar
- 4 tablespoons crushed ice (optional)

To make the agar jelly, put the coconut water in a saucepan and stir in the pandan extract. Add the agar flakes to soak for 30 minutes. Then bring to a very gentle simmer over a low heat without stirring. Once it is bubbling away, add the sugar and stir to dissolve. Cook on a low simmer for about 5 minutes. Pour into a flat vessel like a small baking dish, leave to cool to room temperature then refrigerate. When ready to serve, score the jelly into cubes then remove with a spatula.

To make the sweet bean paste, steam the beans for about 15 minutes. Use a hand-held blender to combine the steamed beans, coconut milk and syrup together into a smooth paste. Set aside.

To make the 'pomegranates', toss the water chestnut cubes in the beetroot juice until all the surfaces are red or pink. Then add the tapioca starch and toss to coat the water chestnuts. Bring a litre of water to the boil in a saucepan then cook the water chestnuts for about 3 minutes or until they float to the top. Drain and rinse with cold water. Set aside.

If using a fresh coconut, break the top of the coconut with a cleaver until you can prise it open enough to fit a tablespoon. Pour the coconut water into a saucepan. Using a spoon, scoop out the coconut flesh into a bowl. If the flesh is hard, slice into thin strips. If soft, leave it.

Add the coconut milk, pandan knots and palm sugar to the pan. Bring to a boil and stir until the sugar dissolves. Let cool to room temperature and refrigerate the infused coconut milk.

When ready to serve, divide the sweet bean paste between 4 tall (Collins) glasses. Then add a layer of agar jelly cubes, then the water chestnuts and the coconut flesh and crushed ice, if using. Pour the infused coconut milk on top and serve with stirrers or long dessert spoons.

Advise your guests to stir the dessert to combine the flavours before digging in.

NOTE

The level of sweetness may differ if using fresh coconut water, as well as between brands. Taste and adjust the sweetness levels of the sweet bean paste.

# MUNG BEAN DUMPLINGS IN SWEET GINGER SYRUP

CHÈ TRÔI NƯỚC

This warm, gingery, sweet soup dessert is another typical favourite Vietnamese *chè*, especially on colder evenings, with soft, smooth and chewy dumplings filled with honeyed, velvety beans. I love the little sticky rice 'marbles' too and making these is always fun, especially with a child or other loved one. The dumplings and 'marbles' can be made way ahead of time and the ginger will become stronger the longer you infuse.

Serves 3–4
Prep time — 20 minutes
Cooking time — 35 minutes

For the dumpling filling

30 g (1 oz) split mung beans, soaked 30 minutes
1 tablespoon desiccated (dried, shredded) coconut
1 tablespoon honey
1 tablespoon coconut milk

For the sweet ginger syrup

250 ml (8½ fl oz/1 cup) coconut water
30 g (1 oz) rock sugar
40 g (1 ½ oz) fresh ginger root, peeled, sliced

For the dumpling dough

100 g (3½ oz) glutinous rice flour, plus extra for dusting
pinch of salt
120 ml (4 fl oz/½ cup) boiling water

For the toppings

drizzle of coconut milk
1 teaspoon toasted sesame seeds
1 tablespoon desiccated coconut

Put the beans in a saucepan with 100 ml (3½ fl oz/scant ½ cup) of water and bring to a boil. Cover, turn the heat down to medium and simmer for about 20 minutes.

In another pan, add the coconut water, sugar and ginger. Bring to a simmer over a medium heat for 5 minutes until the sugar has dissolved. Turn off the heat and let the ginger infuse.

Once the beans are done (they should absorb all the water), mash them with a fork or potato masher then combine with the coconut, honey and coconut milk until it forms a smooth paste. Set the filling aside.

Mix the glutinous rice flour, salt and just-boiled water in a bowl with a wooden spoon, then quickly knead for 5 minutes with your hands. The resulting dough should resemble Play-Doh. Dust your hands with flour if needed.

Dust a clean work surface with flour and roll the dough into a sausage about 3 cm (1 in) in diameter. If the dough seems too wet, add a little flour. If too dry (which will make the balls crack), add a little water. Cut the sausage of dough into 12 pieces, and set three pieces aside, covered in a container.

Take one of the nine remaining pieces of dough and roll it into a ball, then squash it with your palm to get a 5 mm (¼ in) thick disc with a 5 cm (2 in) diameter.

Put a teaspoonful of filling into the middle of the disc then pinch the dough together to form a ball. If it breaks, patch it together and roll with both palms to get a smooth ball. Repeat to form nine filled dumplings. With the three pieces of dough set aside, break each one into four pieces and roll them into 12 marbles.

Bring another saucepan of water to a boil and add the dumplings. After a minute, gently stir them around so that they do not stick to the bottom. Cook for 5 minutes until they float to the top. Once they are there, give them another 1–2 minutes to cook all the way through, then remove the dumplings with a slotted spoon and place them into the pan of sweet ginger syrup.

To serve, gently heat up the pan of sweet ginger syrup and dumplings, serve in a bowl with a dash of coconut milk and the sesame seeds and desiccated coconut.

# BANANA BREAD LAYER CAKE

BÁNH DA LỢN

As kids, we loved making this dessert, it is simple and easily introduces children to baking. It's also perfect for using up ripe bananas and bread that's about to go stale. This recipe is based on the very traditional Vietnamese dessert *bánh chuối hấp*, which uses the baguette insides that are usually torn out when making *bánh mì* (page 127) plus any stale baguette. If you can get little Asian finger bananas, the banana flavour will be more intense.

Serves 6
Prep time — 15 minutes
Cooking time — 45 minutes

160 g (5⅔ oz) condensed milk
300 ml (10 fl oz/1¼ cups) coconut milk
1 teaspoon vanilla extract
¾ French baguette, sliced diagonally with crust or 10 slices of stale white bread, roughly torn
800 g (1 lb 12 oz) ripe bananas (6 standard, i.e., Cavendish)
25 g (¾ oz/2 tablespoons) melted butter or coconut oil
2 teaspoons brown or caster (superfine) sugar

Preheat a fan oven to 180°C (350°F/gas 4).

In a large mixing bowl, combine the condensed milk with the coconut milk and vanilla extract. Add the bread, mix together and submerge to soak.

Peel and cut each of the bananas into thin, diagonal slices.

Grease a 20 cm (8 in) springform cake tin (pan) with the melted butter, sprinkle the inside with 1 teaspoon of the sugar, then fill the tin with one layer of banana slices. Next, arrange a layer of bread, soaked in coconut and condensed milk, on top of the bananas. Flatten the bread with the back of a spoon, then add another layer of banana and another layer of soaked bread. Flatten the bread before adding a last layer of banana. Sprinkle the rest of the sugar on top and bake for 40–45 minutes. Let the cake cool before slicing and serving.

NOTES

Sprinkle with desiccated coconut, almond flakes, walnut or pecan pieces for an extra layer of texture. Feel free to decorate with berries at the bottom or throw in some raisins throughout.

To make this boozy, put a thumb over a bottle of coconut rum and splash it around the cake.

# SOYA MILK

SỮA ĐẬU NÀNH

My mum missed Vietnam so much as a refugee, that she went to extreme lengths to cure her homesickness. At half-term or the summer holidays, we couldn't afford to go away. Instead, my mum found soya beans from Chinatown, soaked them and made my brother and me sit on the kitchen floor and peel the skins off every single bean, hundreds and thousands of them. As she couldn't afford a blender at the time, my mum would then massage the peeled beans with water and milk them with her bare hands for what seemed like hours. The smell of fresh, creamy soya beans is a little thing that reminded us all of home. Thankfully, soya milk can be made quickly and easily now. I enjoy a hot mug a lot of mornings!

Makes 1 litre (34 fl oz/4 cups)
Prep time — 8 minutes
Soaking time — overnight
Cooking time — 30 minutes

100 g (3½ oz) high quality soya beans, soaked overnight, rinsed, drained
1 litre (34 fl oz/4 cups) water
16 g (generous ½ oz) rock sugar (optional)

Add the drained and soaked soya beans to a blender with the water and blend on high speed until it becomes smooth and silky.

Line a sieve with muslin (cheesecloth), set it over a large saucepan, then pour in and strain the milk. Bring the cloth together and squeeze out the milk, then discard the solids in the muslin. Please do not be tempted to try the soya milk at this stage, as it needs to be cooked first before consumption.

Bring the milk in the pan to a gentle boil, watching carefully because it will want to suddenly boil over. Once it looks like it wants to do that, skim off any foam or residue, add the sugar, if using, and cover with a lid. Simmer the milk over a low heat for 20 minutes.

Skim off any other foam or residue and serve the soya milk warm or chilled. Store in the refrigerator for up to 3 days.

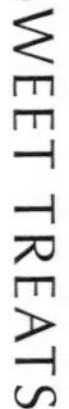

# AVOCADO AND COCONUT SHAKE

SINH TỐ BƠ

Avocado is considered sweet rather than savoury in Vietnam. As my mother didn't own a blender, she made this shake by mashing the avocado with condensed milk or sugar. It would be lumpy, buttery and so delicious. You can be enjoyed like a mousse or fool or even on a baguette. This recipe can also make amazing ice cream by adding an extra tablespoon of condensed milk and churning in an ice cream maker. For special occasions, dress up your shake or ice cream with coconut flesh or cubes of, jackfruit, dragon fruit and so on.

Serves 4
Prep time — 5 minutes

4 ripe avocados, halved
500 ml (17 fl oz/2 cups) coconut water
160 g (5⅔ oz) condensed milk
ice cubes (optional)

Scoop out the flesh of the avocados into a blender. Add the coconut water, condensed milk and ice, if using, and blend everything together.

Serve immediately.

Other combinations to try out

Many vendors open up their shake stands as the sun goes down, as that's when people will tend to pop out for their cooling and healthy(-ish) drinks. Fruit shakes are loved as much as sharing fruit; both are considered gifts to the mouth.

Blend these with a little water or coconut water, add honey or maple syrup to enhance the sweetness. These can also be frozen in moulds to make refreshing ice lollies or served as sorbet.

- papaya and melon
- apple with mint leaves
- soursop and guava
- guava and pineapple
- mango and strawberries
- dragon fruit and lychee
- watermelon with mint leaves

# LIME SODA WITH STRAWBERRIES

SODA DÂU

Sài Gòn, 1980, I was a little girl and it was my birthday. The monsoon rains hit hard on the tin roof and the humidity grew a mist on our faces. My grandmother gave me my first taste of sweet, tart strawberries in the form of *xi rô* (syrup), somehow imported in such a tight embargo. Although Vietnam is now rich with both tropical and non-tropical vegetation, when I was born there, there was a widespread scarcity of food due to war and famine. Nowadays, the country thrives, bursting with refreshing lime sodas, fresh young coconut water, pressed sugar-cane juice and milky iced coffees to quench the thirsty and soothe the sultry heat, as we sit under a ceiling fan or crouched in the shade of a papaya tree. Recipe pictured opposite.

Serves 4
Prep time — 10 minutes

juice of 4 limes
4 tablespoons brown sugar or maple syrup
8 strawberries, sliced
pinch of freshly ground black pepper
ice cubes
800 ml (28 fl oz/3½ cups) sparkling water
½ lime, sliced into 4 wheels

Crush the lime juice and sugar together with a pestle and mortar. Divide this sugar paste into glasses, then crush the strawberries in the mortar and add these. Add the pepper, ice cubes and sparkling water. Serve immediately with lime wheels perched on the rim and stirrers and/or straws.

# LYCHEE, DRAGON FRUIT AND BASIL SEED

HẠT É TRÁI VẢI

Fresh dragon fruit and lychees are rarely in season at the same time, so feel free to use tinned lychees or another fruit in this fun basil-seed drink, commonly consumed for freshness and coolness. Buy the basil seeds (*hạt é*) from the Asian supermarket where they are also known as *sabja* or *takmaria*.

Serves 4
Prep time — 15 minutes

2 tablespoons basil seeds
500 ml (17 fl oz/2 cups) coconut water
230 g (generous 8 oz) fresh or tinned lychees (drained weight)
1 pink or white dragon fruit, cut into bite-size cubes

Soak the basil seeds in the coconut water for at least 5 minutes – they will expand and become jelly-like. Chill in the refrigerator until ready to serve. Add the lychees and dragon fruit just before serving in glasses.

# EIGHT

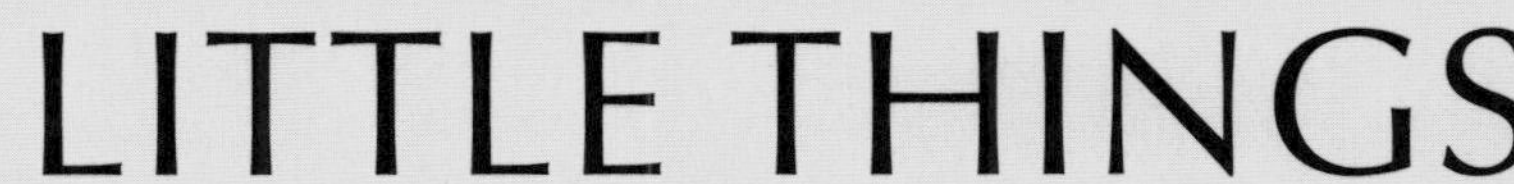

# LITTLE THINGS

# LITTLE THINGS

In all my recipes, I wish to share the tastes of my childhood adapted into a modern vegetarian way to anyone who wishes to cook and eat Vietnamese food. In my mind, I am still that child and teenager who adored my mother's cooking, still sitting at our humble fold-out table, covered by a sticky plastic cloth, patterned with oranges and orange blossoms, in a London council flat. I see her placing pickles into my bowl, a customary gesture of love, and fanning fresh green, blanched leaves over my brother's rice bowl and ladling watercress and ginger soup into mine.

Although I have worked hard to cook, write and test my recipes, I still feel that I will never reach the heights of my quiet, modest and beautiful mother who has spent years perfecting her Vietnamese cooking here in the UK where we have laid down our roots. It transports us back to our motherland and much-loved family in Vietnam, far away.

And although I have replicated and recreated these Vietnamese dishes with a vegetarian twist, my mum is really the person who gave these recipes their true, brilliant and vivid flavours, for I learned the basics from her and followed her palate, before I ventured into using non-traditional ingredients when I started to cook for myself.

My mum always managed to feed us so well on the little money she had. She showed me that cooking from scratch doesn't have to be complex, time-consuming, unsustainable or expensive. It doesn't have to be a chore either, but instead a joyous activity. She taught me that cooking from the heart is the best way to go about it.

Best of all, she taught me that the little things – such as making the perfect fluffy rice and pickles to enhance daily meals to creating pleasurable drinks and tasty broths for satisfying cravings – are the foundations to everything.

# HOMEMADE VEGAN FISH SAUCE



NƯỚC MẮM CHAY

Since I had the honour and privilege of writing this book and testing recipes for it, I have discovered many things that I wouldn't have if I were not researching and writing about vegetarian food. The main challenge was to replace fish sauce in my cooking. Fish sauce is the staple of Vietnamese cooking, giving dishes the unbeatable umami taste that makes our food so stunningly good. In my quest to find a vegan alternative, I looked at several vegan fish sauces on the market and saw that most are soy-based and very salty, but otherwise flavourless, which means it is better to use salt or soy sauce, even if those are not the same. I found Yondu vegetable umami sauce which can be good for salad dressings, but I am not sure if this can be found everywhere, therefore I recommend you try a few different umami pastes and see which ones you like.

It turned out the answer was staring me at the face as I stood in my mother's south-facing herb and vegetable garden. It is invaded by a herb called fish mint (*giấp cá*), which literally tastes like fish with a sour overtone. It is already great raw in salads and wraps, but I found that it is fantastic to brew and make your own vegan fish sauce. It might be a challenge to find this herb, but if you get the chance to grow it yourself in pots, then you can have your own homemade vegan fish sauce practically on tap.

Makes 60 ml (2 fl oz/¼ cup)
Prep time — 10 minutes
Cooking time — 10 minutes

20–30 g (1 oz) fish mint
100 ml (3½ fl oz/scant ½ cup) water
1 tablespoon maple syrup or caster (superfine) sugar
1 teaspoon sea salt
3 garlic cloves
1 bird's eye chilli, whole
1 teaspoon lime juice

Simmer the fish mint leaves in a saucepan over a medium-high heat with the water, maple syrup, salt, garlic and chilli for about 10 minutes until it reduces by half. Discard the leaves, garlic and chilli.

To serve, add the lime juice.

This will only keep for a day before it discolours. It can still be used within a couple of days but it will look murky, so only make what you need.

To make a dipping sauce, adjust accordingly, adding a little hot water if too salty, extra sweetness using sugar and extra sharpness using lime juice.



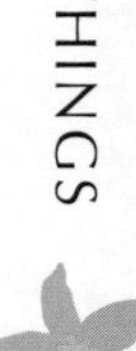

# DUMPLING WRAPPERS

VỎ HÁ CẢO

Dumpling wrappers are available in city-based shops. It is just as easy to make them. I use a pasta machine to roll out the dough, but you can also roll these out by hand with a rolling pin.

Makes 25–30
Prep time — 30 minutes
Resting time — 30 minutes

200 g (7 oz) '00' flour
50 ml (1¾ oz) just-boiled water
60 ml (2 fl oz) cold water

Put the flour into a bowl or free-standing mixer bowl then pour in the just-boiled water and quickly combine together with a spatula until it forms a crumbly texture, then add the cold water. Knead together until it becomes a smooth dough (about 10 minutes).

Rest for 30 minutes in an airtight container, then roll into a sausage. Cut into three equal parts. Keep two of them in an airtight container, while you roll out the first piece.

Using a pasta roller, squash out a piece then put it through the machine about four times at level 1 and lightly dust the sheet. Then run through to level 2. Repeat at each level until you reach level 6. If you don't have a pasta roller, use a rolling pin; place the dough on a lightly floured surface and roll out until it is about 1 mm thick.

Once the sheet is done, place on a lightly floured surface. Using a cookie cutter or even a thin-lipped mug or bowl, cut the dough out into rounds about 8 cm (3 in).

To make the dumplings

Set aside a small bowl of water. Place the wrapper on the palm of your hand, wet the edges with your finger and fill with 2 teaspoons of your chosen filling, then fold the wrapper in half together with your fingers. Use your index finger and thumb to create pleats along the edges, pressing the edges together. You should be able to get about 5–7 pleats in one dumpling. Repeat with the others.

# HOMEMADE VEGETABLE STOCK

NƯỚC DÙNG TỪ RAU CỦ

Having a homemade vegetable stock in the refrigerator for general cooking, such as making a noodle broth, a base for a stew or curry and a splash in a stir-fry makes life easier, speeds up cooking and is much healthier (as you don't have to use stock cubes).

Gather a variety of vegetables, peelings, and odds and ends. Consider the flavour profile of the vegetables; have a mix so that there is sweetness, bitterness, umami, freshness, earthiness and tanginess. The more you can pack into your stockpot, the more layers of flavours can be achieved, but consider what you are going to make with the stock. Perhaps keep the aromatics at bay until it is needed, as they might tarnish the flavours of certain dishes or make it taste muddled. Be mindful of the seasoning; it may be best to keep the stock unseasoned. Keep the stock clear and clean by avoiding vegetables such as starchy potatoes and pumpkins that break down easily, therefore making the stock cloudy and muddy, or scoop them out after 10 minutes. Consider the colour of your vegetables: dried mushrooms will turn the stock brown; beetroot will stain it crimson. Think twice about broccoli and cabbage which can give the stock a sulphurous and bitter flavour. If adding, do so at the end for 5 minutes.

To make a fresh and light stock, add peas, courgette (zucchini) and green beans in the last 5–10 minutes of cooking. To make a richer stock, add dried mushrooms and char or roast certain vegetables to enhance its sweetness and bring out its flavours, such as onion, ginger, daikon, carrot and parsnip.

Sweetness

carrot, parsnip, sweet potato, Asian pear, apple

Bitterness/aniseed

daikon, swede, fennel, celery

Sharpness

pineapple, lemon

Umami/earthy

seaweed, fresh or dried mushrooms, pumpkin peel, butternut squash peel, celeriac, lentils, beans, tomato purée (paste), new potatoes (with skins), onion, shallots, leek, spring onions

Freshness

peas, courgette (zucchini), Turkish/white cabbage, green beans, runner beans, asparagus ends

Aromatics

ginger, lemongrass, garlic, spices, herbs

Cut and slice the vegetables you have chosen into chunks so that there is more surface area for the water to absorb flavours, but not too thin that they break down. Place the prepared vegetables in a stockpot, cover them with water, bring it to a boil and then gently simmer with the lid on for about 30 minutes–1 hour 30 minutes.

Store the stock in a refrigerator in a squeaky-clean container for up to 5 days or freeze for 1 month.

# HOMEMADE BÁNH CANH NOODLES

BÁNH CANH

I saw my friend Jacqueline Clibbon aka @papayaverte make these on Instagram. This is her recipe. She often explores Vietnamese cuisine beautifully to find her roots and I feel it gives her a great sense of belonging. It wasas if she had given me the biggest gift because I often make these noodles which are incredibly, delightful and easy. There is no need to knead with all your might, no need for any fancy machinery and no need for any resting time. I love them in Bánh Canh Noodle Soup (page 144) and Fried Bánh Canh Noodles with Purple Sprouting Broccoli (page 109). These noodles are just the best!

Serves 2–3
Prep time — 15 minutes
Cooking time — 10 minutes

125 g (4 oz) Asian tapioca starch, plus 1 tablespoon for dusting
100 g (3½ oz/scant ⅔ cup) Asian rice flour
160 ml (5½ fl oz/⅔ cup) boiling water

Dust a large, clean work surface with 1 tablespoon of the tapioca starch.

Combine the rest of the tapioca starch and the rice flour in a mixing bowl.

Get a rolling pin, knife, spatula and measuring cup ready. Bring the water to the boil in a kettle.

As soon as the kettle has boiled, quickly measure out the water and pour in a circular motion into the flour mix. Using the spatula, quickly bring the dough together. It will be soft and flaky. After a minute, use your hands to knead the dough together into a smooth Play-Doh-like consistency. Continue to knead on the floured work surface for a couple of minutes, then use a rolling pin to roll out the dough until you get 5 mm (¼ in) thickness. Use a knife or pizza cutter and slice it into 5 mm (¼ in) thick strips. Dust with more flour.

To cook, bring a saucepan of water to a rolling boil over a high heat and add the noodles. After a minute, use a pair of chopsticks to separate the noodles and free them from sticking to the bottom. Simmer for 10 minutes, then have a taste. There should still be some bite. Drain and rinse the noodles with hot water and then portion into noodle soup bowls and serve with Bánh Canh Noodle Soup or any broth you desire.

If you have leftover noodles, keep them refrigerated in an airtight container for up to 3 days. This dough can also be put into a ricer for thinner, round vermicelli noodles.

# CRISPY NOODLES

MÌ XÀO GIÒN

It is best to use a wok or a large deep frying pan (skillet) for this, because the noodles will puff up and need space to do so. It is also advisable to own a thermometer with a clip to attach to your wok, because if the oil is not hot enough, the noodles will not crisp up, or if too hot, then they will burn. It is also really useful to have a large spider to scoop the noodle nests in and out quickly.

50 g (1¾ oz) per person: fresh or dried egg noodles
oil, for deep-frying

If using fresh noodles

Separate and loosen the bundles, then form them into a nest and place onto a plate. Leave it to dry and harden for at least half a day (this ensures a nice bite to the noodles), turning over once and making sure all the strands are loose. Then place it in a heatproof container and pour boiling water over it. Submerge for 3 minutes then drain completely, shaking out any excess water.

If using dried noodles

Place in a saucepan of boiling water. When they become pliable, loosen the bundles with chopsticks and par-boil for about 2 minutes then drain. Leave in the sieve or colander until all the water is drained or shake out the excess water. Take this time to prep the toppings.

To cook

Once the noodles are dried and ready, heat up the oil in a large frying pan (skillet) or wok to 160–180°C (320–350°F). With wooden chopsticks or tongs, take a bundle onto a spider then gently submerge the spider into the hot oil. Release the noodles from the spider and use your chopsticks to spread the noodle strands out into a round nest about 20 cm (8 in). Let it sizzle and bubble for about 30 seconds then turn the noodles over. Once you can feel that the noodles have crisped up (after 30 seconds approximately) and turned golden, take them out of the oil. Transfer the noodles onto a cooling rack to drain the excess oil and cool. You will see that they continue to cook and further turn golden.

Serve with a wet and juicy stir-fry of your choice, such as crispy noodles with all the broccoli (page 110).

NOTES

If you don't have a thermometer, test a very small batch of noodles. Always leave time for the oil to heat up again in between batches.

If you don't have a spider, use a wooden spoon or metal slotted spoon, and spread the noodles once they are in the oil with chopsticks or tongs.



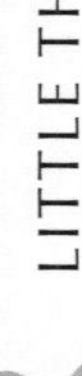

# EGG-FRIED RICE

CƠM CHIÊN TRỨNG

For home comforts or to dress up rice meals and feasts, egg-fried rice is somehow both simple and special. It is as good as what you give it, but knowing when not to overdo it is key too. I actually prefer to use a little sprinkling of mushroom seasoning powder rather than soy sauce, because the rice remains pale but it also delivers a good punch of umami. It is best to use cold, leftover rice, as freshly cooked rice tends to get mushy in the pan. I do like to enjoy a bowl with an extra fried egg on top and lots of Maggi liquid seasoning.

Prep time — 5 minutes
Cooking time — 7 minutes

a little ghee or rapeseed (canola) oil
1–2 garlic cloves, roughly sliced
cold, cooked rice
mushroom seasoning powder or soy sauce or a little of both
spring onions (scallions), sliced
freshly ground black pepper
1–2 eggs

For the additional options

Maggi liquid seasoning, peas, sweetcorn, carrot, edamame beans, Pickled Mustard Greens (page 207), kimchi, Crispy Shallots (page 208), mushrooms, coriander (cilantro) leaves, chives, curry powder

In a hot wok, add the ghee with garlic. Add the cooked rice as soon as the garlic starts to colour and stir-fry with the seasoning, spring onion and black pepper. Fold it all together, then make a well at the centre of the wok. Crack in your egg(s), let it sit for 30 seconds, then stir up the egg with your cooking utensil. Let it cook 30 seconds longer, then combine with the rice and vigorously stir-fry until done.

NOTES

If using frozen vegetables like peas and edamame, fry them at the start with the garlic for a minute or so or until they thaw.

If using tinned sweetcorn, pickles or kimchi, I like adding them after the egg stage along with any herbs like coriander (cilantro) or chives.



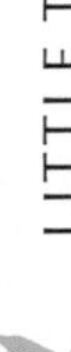

# PERFECT STEAMED RICE

CƠM

A meal isn't considered a real meal in Vietnamese culture unless it comes with rice. Respect your rice. It is a staple, it makes the meal complete, and if it's made well, you will enjoy your food a lot more.

For Vietnamese jasmine rice, I use approximately 300 g (10½ oz/1½ cups) of rice and 500 ml (17 fl oz/2 cups) of water (serves 3–4). Wash the rice first – about three times in its cooking pot – running your fingers through the grains and slightly massaging them to release the starch. Then pour away the starchy water using the palm of your hands to stop the grains from falling (or use a sieve). Fill the pot with 1.5–2 cm (⅔–¾ in) of water above the rice.

To cook rice, there is no better way to do it than in a basic rice cooker. When the rice is cooked, fluff it up with a wooden or plastic paddle or spatula, by mixing and turning it around, then leave the rice to rest and fluff up in the cooker for a further 5–10 minutes.

If you don't have a rice cooker, cook the rice in a saucepan with a lid on medium–low heat. After 5 minutes, when the water has seeped into the rice and there isn't any water on the surface, turn the heat down to low and cook with the lid securely on to let the steam do its work for a further 15–18 minutes. Then turn off the heat without removing the lid and let it rest for 5–10 minutes, before fluffing up the rice with a rice paddle or wooden spoon. (You will often get a crispy or burnt bottom this way which is a treat in itself.) The aim is to get fluffy, cooked-just-right rice that isn't sticking together in clumps, too soft and watery or hard and chalky. Your rice is perfect when you can sink your teeth into it and it has a lovely, mild nutty and floral flavour.

# TRADITIONAL VIETNAMESE PICKLES

ĐỒ CHUA NGÂM GIÒN

Makes 400–600 g (14 oz–1 lb 5 oz)
Prep time — 50 minutes
Cooking time — 5 minutes

2 carrots, peeled
10 cm (4 in) chunk of daikon, peeled
1 kohlrabi, peeled
2 garlic cloves (optional)
3 tablespoons sea salt
100 ml (3½ fl oz/scant ½ cup) water
100 ml (3½ fl oz/scant ½ cup) cider vinegar
7 tablespoons caster (superfine) sugar
2–3 bird's eye chillies

Cut the carrots at a diagonal (to give length) into 5 mm (¼ in) slices, then use a crinkle cutter to cut further into 5 mm (¼ in) pieces. Do the same with the daikon and kohlrabi.

Place the vegetables and garlic, if using, in a bowl with the salt and submerge with water for 30 minutes. Rinse really well and drain in a colander for 15 minutes. Then pack the vegetables into a large, sterilised jar.

To make the pickle brine, boil the water with the vinegar and sugar, then let cool to room temperature and pour onto the packed vegetables and bird's eye chillies in the jar. Pickle for 1–2 days at room temperature, then refrigerate and keep for up to 2 weeks.

NOTE

The same can be done with a cucumber for a quick pickle. Use a peeler to create ribbons and 2 round shallots, thinly sliced. Use half of everything else.

# INSTANT CARROT AND DAIKON PICKLE

ĐỒ CHUA

Makes 200 g (7 oz)
Prep time — 10 minutes
Pickling time — 30 minutes

100 g (3½ oz) carrot, thinly sliced or julienned
100 g (3½ oz) daikon, thinly sliced or julienned
1½ tablespoons caster (superfine) sugar
2 tablespoons cider vinegar

In a mixing bowl, combine the carrot, daikon, sugar and vinegar. For sliced vegetables, leave for 30 minutes or more to pickle, for julienned, leave for 15 minutes. The thicker the vegetable, the longer you need.

NOTE

For a fun touch, use a peeler to thinly slice rounds of candied and golden beetroot (beets) and make an instant pickle, or slice into thick matchsticks for the typical pickle.

# PICKLED MUSTARD GREENS

CẢI CHUA

Mustard greens are great, fresh or pickled. I love their unique bitter flavour. This pickle has the perfect combination of sweet, sour, bitter and heat. It retains a certain crunch as well. Pickled greens are commonplace at the Vietnamese table; their job is to balance out all the savouriness, like a pick-me-up or a much-needed sidekick to rice meals.

Makes 300 g (10½ oz)
Prep time — 10 minutes

250 g (9 oz) mustard greens
500 ml (17 fl oz/2 cups) just-boiled water
10 g (⅓ oz) sea salt
45 g (1¾ oz/3 tablespoons) sugar
2 garlic cloves
2 chillies
1 tablespoon cider vinegar

Slice the leafy ends of the mustard greens into 10 cm (4 in) pieces and the paler stalks into 5 cm (2 in) pieces. Wash the leaves and dry thoroughly.

Bring a kettle to the boil and add the water to a measuring jug with the salt, sugar, garlic, chillies and vinegar. Set aside this pickle brine to cool enough that you can touch it.

Meanwhile, clean a jar really well with soap and water, then sterilise it by filling it to the brim with boiling hot water for 10 minutes before draining.

Pack the sliced greens into the jar then submerge with the pickle brine, making sure there are no air pockets. Seal tight with the lid.

Keep in a warm dark place for 2–4 days, opening the lid every day to 'burp' any air. The greens are ready once they turn from vibrant green to a dull mustard green. You can also taste it to see if it is sour to your liking.

# CRISPY THINGS

Ideas for salads, noodles, rice and snacking.

Rice crackers

Deep-fry rice-paper sheets at 180°C (350°F) for a few seconds. As soon as they puff up, take them out of the oil and drain on paper towels. You can make fun decorations by cutting out flowers and shape.

Crispy rice noodles

Make lovely, puffy, crispy noodles by placing a small bundle of dry (uncooked) rice vermicelli in hot oil and watch the magic. These are fabulous sprinkled on salads.

# CRISPY SHALLOTS

HÀNH PHI

These are used as toppings to elevate any dish, but they also flavour broths remarkably well. Recipe pictured opposite.

Makes approx. 300 g (10½ oz)
Prep time — 15 minutes
Cooking time — 15 minutes

4 tablespoons vegetable oil
12 round shallots, thinly sliced

Heat the oil in a frying pan (skillet) over a low heat and fry the shallot until golden, then remove from the heat and drain on paper towels (saving the flavoured oil). They will continue to brown and crisp. Save the shallot oil and crispy shallots in two separate containers for future use with noodle soups and to garnish rice, noodles and salads.

# CORIANDER PESTO

NUÔI SỐT NGÒ

This makes a luxurious dip for crudités, is great slathered in a bánh mì tossed with blanched vegetables and tofu, or used to dress salad and of course wonderful on pasta or noodles.

Serves 4
Prep time — 10 minutes

30 g (1 oz) desiccated (dried shredded) coconut, pine nuts, cashews, almonds, pistachios or peanuts
60 g (2 oz) coriander (cilantro), with stalks, snipped into 3 cm (1 in) lengths
4 tablespoons avocado oil, walnut oil or groundnut (peanut) oil, plus extra for topping
4 tablespoons nutritional yeast
zest and juice of ½ lemon or lime
1 teaspoon sea salt
2 garlic cloves, sliced

Put all the ingredients in a bowl or small blender and (hand) blend together until it forms a smooth, pale green pesto.

Place in a clean, sterilised jar and add 5 mm (¼ in) of oil on top to conserve the pesto.

Serve spread over slices of baguette or slathered on homemade noodles

Keep refrigerated and consume within 5 days.

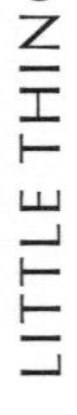

# SPRING ONION OIL

MỠ HÀNH

Fragrant and flavoursome, this is used throughout the book to add essential colour and character to vegetables and noodles.

Makes approx. 80 ml (2¾ fl oz/⅓ cup)
Prep time — 15 minutes
Cooking time — 3–5 minutes

4 tablespoons oil
5 spring onions (scallions), white and green parts, sliced
pinch of sea salt

Put the oil and spring onion in a small saucepan over a low heat and cook with the salt, stirring occasionally, for 3 minutes until the spring onion softens, then remove from the heat.

NOTE

Save spring onion rooted ends in a glass of water and regrow. Change the water every other day.

# LEMONGRASS AND CHILLI OIL

SA TẾ

Making a batch of this is really valuable when you're super-busy because adding a teaspoon to a vegetable broth can transform its subtlety into a zingy bowl, full of spice and umami. It's also great to marinade tofu, throw into a stir-fry or use as a condiment on all your favourite dishes.

Makes approx. 100 ml (3½ fl oz/scant ½ cup)
Prep time — 5–15 minutes
Cooking time — 15 minutes

5 garlic cloves
3 shallots
4 lemongrass stalks, finely chopped
1 tablespoon neutral cooking oil
2 teaspoons chilli powder or chilli (hot pepper) flakes
2 teaspoons sea salt
2 teaspoons brown sugar
1 teaspoon mushroom seasoning powder
2 tablespoons shop-bought crispy chilli oil
2 tablespoons rapeseed (canola) oil

In a grinder or small food processor, blend the garlic, shallots and lemongrass together. If you don't have a machine, finely chop by hand.

Place in a frying pan (skillet) with the cooking oil and cook over a medium heat for 7–10 minutes until golden. Then reduce to a low heat, add the chilli powder, salt, sugar, mushroom seasoning powder and crispy chilli oil. Mix well together, then cook for another 5 minutes, stirring occasionally. Turn off the heat, let it cool uncovered, then transfer to a sterilised jar and cover the top with the rapeseed oil.

Refrigerate and use within 3 weeks.

# DIPPING SAUCES AND DRESSINGS

NƯỚC CHẤM

The trick to making a tasty sauce is to get the right balance of sweet, sour, salty, umami, bitter and spiciness. Always taste when you are making sauces (or anything) so that you can get the balance spot on. Remember that all brands of condiments will vary from one to another so use these recipes as a guide. Some can be mixed or shaken, or you can use a mortar and pestle. It's completely up to you. Where I use oil or ghee, gently cook the garlic/shallots and all the ingredients together. To make your own sauces, you can use anything you have, like preserves and jams for sweetness, vinegar for sour if limes or lemons are unavailable. Simply go with the five flavour profiles to meet the perfect balance.

## Buttery apricot sauce

1 tablespoon ghee
1 garlic clove, finely chopped
2 bird's eye chillies, finely chopped
1 tablespoon apricot jam
1 tablespoon Homemade Vegan Fish Sauce (page 193)

## Sweet lime sauce

juice of ½ lime
2 tablespoons sugar
2 tablespoons Homemade Vegan Fish Sauce (page 193) or soy sauce
1 bird's eye chilli, sliced thinly at a diagonal

## Ginger and lime sauce

1 teaspoon mustard
1 tablespoon ginger preserve
¾ tablespoon soy sauce
2 teaspoons lime juice
1 bird's eye chilli, finely chopped

## Red onion vinegar

1 red onion, sliced thinly into 3 mm (⅛ in) half-moons
1 tablespoon cider vinegar
1 teaspoon freshly ground black pepper
1 teaspoon maple syrup
1 tablespoon Homemade Vegan Fish Sauce (page 193)
1 tablespoon avocado oil or rapeseed (canola) oil
1 teaspoon sesame oil

## Passion fruit, lemon and honey dressing

½ tablespoon soy sauce
1 passion fruit, pulp only
½ tablespoon honey
1 bird's eye chilli, finely sliced
zest and juice of ½ lemon

## Salad dressing

2 tablespoons maple syrup
3 tablespoons Homemade Vegan Fish Sauce (page 193)
3 tablespoons lime juice, plus zest of 1 lime
2 garlic cloves, crushed
1 bird's eye chilli, finely chopped
3 tablespoons shelled pistachios or salted, roasted peanuts, coarsely chopped or crushed

## Marmalade and mustard dressing

1 green bird's eye chilli
1 teaspoon fermented tofu
1 tablespoon perilla sauce, soy sauce or Homemade Vegan Fish Sauce (page 193)
1 teaspoon English mustard
1 teaspoon marmalade

### Mango and mint dressing

1 bird's eye chilli, finely chopped
1 garlic clove, crushed
2 tablespoons mango chutney
2 tablespoons Yondu vegetable umami sauce
finely chopped zest and juice of ½ lime or lemon
10 g (⅓ oz) mint leaves, finely chopped

### Nước mắm (traditional Vietnamese dipping sauce)

2 tablespoons Homemade Vegan Fish Sauce (page 193)
1 bird's eye chilli, finely chopped
1 garlic clove, finely chopped
2 tablespoons cider vinegar, or lemon or lime juice with their zest
2 tablespoons agave syrup, maple syrup or caster (superfine) sugar
100 ml (3½ fl oz/scant ½ cup) hot water

### Tahini soy dressing

4 tablespoons soy sauce or light soy sauce
1 tablespoon tahini
juice of ¼ lime or lemon
1 teaspoon maple syrup

### Dipping sauce

2½ tablespoons marmalade
3 teaspoons English mustard
2½ tablespoons soy sauce
juice of ¾ lime (about 2 tablespoons)

### Soy, tahini and crispy chilli oil

2 tablespoons soy sauce
1 tablespoon tahini
1 tablespoon shop-bought crispy chilli oil
1 tablespoon maple syrup or agave syrup
finely chopped zest and juice of ½ lime or lemon

### Ginger soy sauce

40 g (1½ oz) fresh ginger root, peeled, finely chopped
1 garlic clove, finely chopped
½ red chilli or chillies of choice, finely chopped
2 tablespoons soy sauce or Homemade Vegan Fish Sauce (page 193)
1 teaspoon caster (superfine) sugar

### Hoisin and peanut butter dipping sauce

1 teaspoon vegetable oil
1 garlic clove, finely chopped
1 bird's eye chilli, finely chopped
2 tablespoons hoisin sauce
½ tablespoon white wine vinegar or cider vinegar
1 teaspoon caster (superfine) sugar
1 tablespoon water
1 heaped tablespoon smooth or crunchy peanut butter (optional)
2 tablespoons peanuts, cashews or pistachios, crushed or blended (optional)

Heat the oil in a small saucepan over a medium heat. Fry the garlic until it browns slightly, then add the chilli, hoisin sauce, vinegar, sugar, water and peanut butter, if using. Stir together and bring to a gentle boil. Leave the sauce to cool, then pour into dipping bowls and sprinkle crushed nuts on top, if using.

# MIDWEEK MENU

| | |
|---|---|
| Tofu and Tomatoes with Spinach and Basil | 70 |
| Asparagus Egg Terrine | 55 |
| Easy Greens Stir-fried with Garlic | 40 |
| Watercress, Ginger and Silken Tofu Soup | 157 |
| Egg-fried Rice or Perfect Steamed Rice | 202–203 |
| Banana, Coconut and Tapioca Pudding | 168 |

# WEEKEND FEASTING MENU

| | |
|---|---|
| Tofu Knot 'Chicken Wings' | 30 |
| Blood Orange, Grilled Peach and Tomato Salad | 82 |
| Vegetable Spring Rolls | 118 |
| Tapioca Dumplings with Sweet Lime | 25 |
| Mushroom and Tofu Phở | 142 |
| Asparagus Rice-Noodle Rolls with Mushrooms and Pumpkin | 124 |
| Pandan Baked Burnt Basque Cheesecake | 164 |

| | |
|---|---|
| Savoury Pancake Bites | 120 |
| Lemongrass Tofu | 65 |
| Black Bean Aubergines | 50 |
| King Oyster Mushroom and Turmeric Rice | 130 |
| Sweet and Sour Tomato and Golden Beetroot Soup | 154 |
| Rainbow Dessert | 176 |

# ABOUT THE AUTHOR

Uyen Luu is a food photographer. She runs a Vietnamese supper club, as well as cooking classes in her studio in Hackney. Uyen grew up in London, since her family moved there in the 80s as refugees. This is her third book.

www.uyenluu.com
Instagram
@loveleluu

# ACKNOWLEDGEMENTS

Thank you to Kajal Mistry and all at Hardie Grant for commissioning this cookbook; I am honoured to sit among your wonderful and beautiful collection of books. It has been so lovely to work closely with my editor Eila Purvis to pursue delicious recipes I can truly be proud of.

My thanks to MiMi Aye for copy-editing the manuscript. Thank you to my sister-in-law My Lưu for the Vietnamese translation and for always answering my random Vietnamese food and culture questions, and also to my brother Vu for always cooking up a feast for the family.

Thank you with my biggest embrace to my gorgeous food stylists Sam Dixon and Lucy Turnball, as well as Tamara Vos and Florence Blair and props stylist Louie Waller, for the beautiful plates and bowls of food. Clarissa Hulse for fabrics.

Photography shoots are fun but it is stirred with lots of pressure and I would be lost with my faithful assistant Laurie Noble, who kindly looks after me and the photography. Thank you for my lovely portraits too.

Thank you to Evi-O Studio and Susan Le for always coming up with the most incredible designs. You have really captured the essence of my recipes; I am so lucky to have you.

I worked closely with many home cooks who found me via my previous book, *Vietnamese*, from kitchens all over the world. Thank you from the bottom of my heart to those who tested the recipes. I loved waking up in the mornings and discovering your return messages. The dedication and painstaking way you tried to get ingredients, and how you interpret instructions are incredibly valuable to help others achieve these recipes at home. I loved the many compliments I received, and any fails helped me re-evaluate my writing. I loved how I got to know you through recipes and cooking. There were too many to mention, but my special thanks go to Ine Todts, Tamara Mann, Denise De Klein, Cyndi Clinker, Simone Rizik, Lisa Dick, Caroline Lemieux, Christine Twyman, Marlene Parkes, Mary Sargent, Andrea Halsall, Inga Aksamit, Gillian Anderton, Alicia Clyde, Catherine Dallaire, Jules Roberts and Jennie Allen.

My heartfelt thanks without end goes to Jamie Oliver for your kindness, openness and friendship. You've always got a hand to give and I will always cook for you. I appreciate you so much!

Thank you to Allan Jenkins and Molly Tait-Hyland at *Observer Food Monthly* for commissioning my recipes in your wonderful supplement, a space I am most grateful and proud to be in.

Thank you to Huong Black @mrshuongblack and Jacqui Clibbon @papayaverte for inspiring me on a daily basis, seeing the Vietnamese food you cook for your family. I share and admire your sense of tradition kneaded with food discoveries and possibilities. I learn so much from you and I crave to belong like you do, as well as to learn that it is often at the Vietnamese table.

Thank you to my work husbands, Ben Ridolfi and Phil Derham at Park District. Not only do you keep hiring me to work with you (even when I am all upside down and inside out) in between my writing and cooking. You love me like a sister. Whether I am happy or sad, you've got me like I've got you. This means the absolute world.

My love for cooking and eating together stems from my many friendships and moments that will always stay with me. I am so happy that I can now help some of my vegetarian friends Anja Siemens and Camille Sanson enjoy Vietnamese, and those who aren't see how wonderful we can eat with just plants. I am sad to say I haven't been able to see many friends in the last few years, but I write recipes because I know they would really enjoy them. It is like they've seeped into my heart and marinated my soul.

Thank you to my lovely mum and dad friends for making my mornings brighter; Yasmin (and Darya) Moghadam and Anna Matthews. Thank you to Pam and Paul Williams for being great grandparents to Olive. All my love and gratitude to my family in the US: Brian, Jocelyn and Kathleen Luu, chú Hiển and cô Vân who are always there despite the distance. My beloved cousins in Vietnam who I miss tremendously: Thảo, Thúy, Già and Bin.

Thank you to my mum, an inspirational, hardworking force of nature with the biggest heart. Anyone whose ever been to my cooking classes or supper club will know this by her incredible cooking. I love you so much and thank you for always always being a great mother and grandmother.

My greatest thanks and love to James O Jenkins, for all my morning cups of tea, clearing up after all my mess and being the most wonderful and loving father to our daughter Olive and dog Berry. Thank you for giving me time to write and love you give to our little family. I love you.

This book is dedicated to my beautiful daughter Olive Luu Jenkins, for every breath that I breathe is for you. Everything I write is for you to keep as layers of history and belonging. I hope you will always be at home wherever you go in the future with these recipes. I love you with all of my heart.

# INDEX


## A

**apples**
- green papaya salad with pomelo, apple and artichoke 80

**apricot jam**
- buttery apricot sauce 212
- tofu knot 'chicken wings' 30

aromatics 14

**artichokes**
- asparagus rice-noodle rolls with mushrooms and pumpkin 124
- assorted summer rolls 87
- green papaya salad with pomelo, apple and artichoke 80
- lemongrass vegetable and pasta stew 134
- vegetable spring rolls 118

**asparagus**
- asparagus egg terrine 55
- asparagus rice-noodle rolls with mushrooms and pumpkin 124
- cabbage, tofu and kimchi dumplings 21
- rice paper pizza 34
- stuffed courgette-flower salad with aubergine, peas and tofu 84
- vegetable curry puffs 28
- vegetable spring rolls 118

**aubergines**
- black bean aubergines 50
- grilled aubergines with spring onion oil 49
- roasted cauliflower and aubergine dumplings 22
- spiced tofu with aubergine and enoki mushrooms 66
- stuffed courgette-flower salad with aubergine, peas and tofu 84

avocado and coconut shake 184

## B

**baguettes**
- banana bread layer cake 180
- omelette bánh mì 127

**bamboo shoots**
- pumpkin and chickpea curry 133

**banana leaves**
- vegan Vietnamese sausage 117

**bananas**
- banana bread layer cake 180
- banana, coconut and tapioca pudding 168

bánh canh noodle soup 144

**basil**
- tofu and tomatoes with spinach and basil 70

**batter**
- asparagus rice-noodle rolls with mushrooms and pumpkin 124
- tofu knot 'chicken wings' 30

**bean sprouts**
- bean sprouts with samphire 44
- crispy vegetable crêpes 122
- flat rice noodles with bean sprouts and garlic chives 102
- fried bánh canh noodles with purple sprouting broccoli 109
- vegetable spring rolls 118

**beancurd**
- vegan Vietnamese sausage 117

**beetroot**
- sweet and sour tomato and golden beetroot soup 154

**betel leaves**
- sweet potato and celeriac chips wrapped in betel leaves 88

black bean aubergines 50

**broccoli**
- crispy noodles with all the broccoli 110
- fried bánh canh noodles with purple sprouting broccoli 109
- stuffed courgette-flower salad with aubergine, peas and tofu 84

## C

**cabbage**
- cabbage, tofu and kimchi dumplings 21
- lemongrass vegetable and pasta stew 134
- sweet potato noodles with roasted fennel and sweetheart cabbage 95
- vegetable spring rolls 118

**cakes**
- banana bread layer cake 180
- pandan 'birthday' cake 174

**capers**
- stuffed tomatoes with tofu, mushrooms and capers 68
- water spinach with capers 43

**carrots**
- crispy noodles with all the broccoli 110
- green papaya salad with pomelo, apple and artichoke 80
- instant carrot and daikon pickle 204
- lemongrass vegetable and pasta stew 134
- mixed vegetable curry 56
- tapioca dumplings with sweet lime 25
- traditional Vietnamese pickles 204
- vegetable curry puffs 28
- vegetable spring rolls 118

**cauliflower**
- mixed vegetable curry 56
- roasted cauliflower and aubergine dumplings 22
- sweet and sour cauliflower 46
- sweet potato and water chestnut wontons 27
- tapioca dumplings with sweet lime 25
- vegetable curry puffs 28

cavolo nero noodles 96

**celeriac**
- sweet potato and celeriac chips wrapped in betel leaves 88

**celery**
- lemongrass vegetable and pasta stew 134
- sweet and sour vegetable stir-fry 58

**chickpeas**
pumpkin and chickpea curry 133
**chillies**
grilled aubergines with spring onion oil 49
mixed vegetable curry 56
tofu knot 'chicken wings' 30
turmeric and dill tofu 128
watermelon and strawberry salad with chilli salt 78
**coconut**
rainbow dessert 176
**coconut milk**
banana bread layer cake 180
banana, coconut and tapioca pudding 168
lotus and purple sweet potato rice pudding 171
mixed vegetable curry 56
pandan & coconut 'birthday' cake 174
pandan baked burnt Basque cheesecake 164
rainbow dessert 176
**coconut water**
avocado and coconut shake 184
lemongrass tofu 65
lychee, dragon fruit and basil seed 186
mung bean dumplings in sweet ginger syrup 179
pandan & coconut 'birthday' cake 174
spiced tofu with aubergine and enoki mushrooms 66
sweet potato noodles with roasted fennel and sweetheart cabbage 95
**coffee**
Vietnamese coffee ice cream 167
**coriander**
coriander pesto 208
quick and lazy drenched cold noodles 106
**courgette flowers**
stuffed courgette-flower salad with aubergine, peas and tofu 84
**courgettes**
courgette spaghetti with miso and nori 98
crispy vegetable crêpes 122
mango and melon salad with pomelo 77
mixed vegetable curry 56
sweet and sour cauliflower 46
sweet and sour vegetable stir-fry 58
**cream**
Vietnamese coffee ice cream 167
**cream cheese**
pandan baked burnt Basque cheesecake 164
**cucumber**
sweet and sour vegetable stir-fry 58

## D

**daikon**
instant carrot and daikon pickle 204
traditional Vietnamese pickles 204
dipping sauces 212–13
**dough sticks**
Vietnamese dough sticks 32
**dragon fruit**
lychee, dragon fruit and basil seed 186
dressings 212–13
**drinks**
avocado and coconut shake 184
lime soda with strawberries 186
lychee, dragon fruit and basil seed 186
soya milk 183
**dumplings**
cabbage, tofu and kimchi dumplings 21
dumpling wrappers 195
mung bean dumplings in sweet ginger syrup 179
roasted cauliflower and aubergine dumplings 22
tapioca dumplings with sweet lime 25

## E

**eggs**
asparagus egg terrine 55
egg and tomato noodle soup 151
egg and tomato scramble 52
egg-fried rice 202
omelette bánh mì 127
pandan & coconut 'birthday' cake 174
rice paper pizza 34
southern noodle soup 146

## F

**fennel**
sweet potato noodles with roasted fennel and sweetheart cabbage 95
**'fish' sauce**
homemade vegan fish sauce 193
flavours 14
fruity trifle 172

## G

**garlic**
easy greens stir-fried with garlic 40
**garlic chives**
flat rice noodles with bean sprouts and garlic chives 102
ginger soy sauce 213
**goyza**
cabbage, tofu and kimchi dumplings 21
roasted cauliflower and aubergine dumplings 22
**green beans**
mixed vegetable curry 56
savoury pancake bites 120
**greens**
bánh canh noodle soup 144
easy greens stir-fried with garlic 40

## H

**herbs 14**
assorted summer rolls 87
hoisin and peanut butter dipping sauce 213

## I

**ice cream**
Vietnamese coffee ice cream 167
ingredients 12, 14

## K

**kale**
crispy vegetable crêpes 122
**kimchi**
cabbage, tofu and kimchi dumplings 21
crispy vegetable crêpes 122
**kohlrabi**
green papaya salad with pomelo, apple and artichoke 80
traditional Vietnamese pickles 204

## L

**leeks**
asparagus egg terrine 55
asparagus rice-noodle rolls with mushrooms and pumpkin 124
roasted cauliflower and aubergine dumplings 22
vegetable spring rolls 118
**lemongrass**
lemongrass and chilli oil 210
lemongrass noodle soup 148
lemongrass tofu 65
lemongrass vegetable and pasta stew 134
**lemons**
black bean aubergines 50
**lettuce**
assorted summer rolls 87
**limes**
ginger and lime sauce 212
grilled aubergines with spring onion oil 49
lime soda with strawberries 186
salad dressing 212
sweet lime sauce 212
tapioca dumplings with sweet lime 25
lotus and purple sweet potato rice pudding 171
lychee, dragon fruit and basil seed 186

## M

**mangetout**
crispy chilli tofu noodles 100
sweet and sour cauliflower 46
**mangoes**
mango and melon salad with pomelo 77
mango and mint dressing 213
marmalade and mustard dressing 212
**melons**
mango and melon salad with pomelo 77
winter melon stir-fry with tofu and glass noodles 104
**miso**
courgette spaghetti with miso and nori 98
**mung beans**
mung bean dumplings in sweet ginger syrup 179
rainbow dessert 176
savoury pancake bites 120
**mushrooms**
asparagus rice-noodle rolls with mushrooms and pumpkin 124
assorted summer rolls 87
king oyster mushroom and turmeric rice 130
mixed vegetable curry 56
mushroom and tofu pho 142
quick mushroom noodle soup 153
savoury pancake bites 120
spiced tofu with aubergine and enoki mushrooms 66
stuffed tomatoes with tofu, mushrooms and capers 68
sweet and sour cauliflower 46
**mustard greens**
pickled mustard greens 207

## N

**noodles**
asparagus egg terrine 55
asparagus rice-noodle rolls with mushrooms and pumpkin 124
assorted summer rolls 87
bánh canh noodle soup 144
cavolo nero noodles 96
crispy chilli tofu noodles 100
crispy noodles 200
crispy noodles with all the broccoli 110
crispy rice noodles 208
egg and tomato noodle soup 151
flat rice noodles with bean sprouts and garlic chives 102
fried bánh canh noodles with purple sprouting broccoli 109
homemade bánh canh noodles 198
lemongrass noodle soup 148
mushroom and tofu pho 142
quick and lazy drenched cold noodles 106
quick mushroom noodle soup 153
southern noodle soup 146
sweet potato noodles with roasted fennel and sweetheart cabbage 95
vermicelli noodle salad bowls 137
winter melon stir-fry with tofu and glass noodles 104
**nori**
bean sprouts with samphire 44
courgette spaghetti with miso and nori 98

## O

**okra**
tapioca dumplings with sweet lime 25
**olives**
watermelon and strawberry salad with chilli salt 78
omelette bánh mì 127
**onions**
king oyster mushroom and turmeric rice 130
red onion vinegar 212
sweet and sour vegetable stir-fry 58
orange, grilled peach and tomato salad 82

## P

**pancakes**
crispy vegetable crêpes 122
savoury pancake bites 120
**pandan**
pandan & coconut 'birthday' cake 174
pandan baked burnt Basque cheesecake 164
**papaya**
green papaya salad with pomelo, apple and artichoke 80
**passion fruit**
mango and melon salad with pomelo 77
passion fruit, lemon and honey dressing 212
**pasta**
lemongrass vegetable and pasta stew 134
**pastries**
vegetable curry puffs 28
**peaches**
orange, grilled peach and tomato salad 82
**peanuts**
sweet potato and celeriac chips wrapped in betel leaves 88
**peas**
cabbage, tofu and kimchi dumplings 21
lemongrass vegetable and pasta stew 134
stuffed courgette-flower salad with aubergine, peas and tofu 84
**peppers**
spiced tofu with aubergine and enoki mushrooms 66
sweet and sour cauliflower 46
**pesto**
coriander pesto 208
**pickles**
instant carrot and daikon pickle 204
pickled mustard greens 207
traditional Vietnamese pickles 204
**pineapple**
sweet and sour cauliflower 46
sweet and sour vegetable stir-fry 58
**'pizza'**
rice paper pizza 34
**pomegranate**
green papaya salad with pomelo, apple and artichoke 80
**pomelo**
green papaya salad with pomelo, apple and artichoke 80
mango and melon salad with pomelo 77
**potatoes**
lemongrass vegetable and pasta stew 134
mixed vegetable curry 56
pumpkin and chickpea curry 133
vegetable curry puffs 28
**pumpkins**
asparagus rice-noodle rolls with mushrooms and pumpkin 124
pumpkin and chickpea curry 133

## Q

**quail's eggs**
rice paper pizza 34
southern noodle soup 146

## R

rainbow dessert 176
**rice**
any veg rice porridge 158
egg-fried rice 202
king oyster mushroom and turmeric rice 130
lotus and purple sweet potato rice pudding 171
perfect steamed rice 203
**rice paper**
assorted summer rolls 87
rice crackers 208
rice paper pizza 34
vegetable spring rolls 118



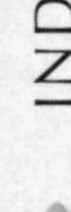

## S

**salads** 75
assorted summer rolls 87
green papaya salad with pomelo, apple and artichoke 80
mango and melon salad with pomelo 77
orange, grilled peach and tomato salad 82
stuffed courgette-flower salad with aubergine, peas and tofu 84
vermicelli noodle salad bowls 137
watermelon and strawberry salad with chilli salt 78
salt and pepper tofu 62
**samphire**
bean sprouts with samphire 44
**sauces**
dipping sauces 212–13
homemade vegan fish sauce 193
**sausages**
vegan Vietnamese sausage 117
**sesame seeds**
courgette spaghetti with miso and nori 98
lemongrass tofu 65
**shallots**
crispy shallots 208
turmeric and dill tofu 128
soup 141
soy, tahini and crispy chilli oil 213
soya milk 183
**spaghetti**
courgette spaghetti with miso and nori 98
**spinach**
tofu and tomatoes with spinach and basil 70
water spinach with capers 43
**spring onions**
crispy noodles with all the broccoli 110
grilled aubergines with spring onion oil 49
omelette bánh mì 127
spring onion oil 210
**spring rolls**
vegetable spring rolls 118
**strawberries**
lime soda with strawberries 186
watermelon and strawberry salad with chilli salt 78
**sugar snap peas**
green papaya salad with pomelo, apple and artichoke 80
tapioca dumplings with sweet lime 25
sweet and sour cauliflower 46
sweet and sour tomato and golden beetroot soup 154
sweet and sour vegetable stir-fry 58
**sweet potatoes**
lotus and purple sweet potato rice pudding 171
sweet potato and celeriac chips wrapped in betel leaves 88
sweet potato and water chestnut wontons 27
sweet potato noodles with roasted fennel and sweetheart cabbage 95
**sweetcorn**
crispy noodles with all the broccoli 110

## T

tahini soy dressing 213
**tapioca**
banana, coconut and tapioca pudding 168
tapioca dumplings with sweet lime 25
**tofu** 61
asparagus egg terrine 55
assorted summer rolls 87
cabbage, tofu and kimchi dumplings 21
crispy chilli tofu noodles 100
crispy noodles with all the broccoli 110
lemongrass noodle soup 148
lemongrass tofu 65
lemongrass vegetable and pasta stew 134
mushroom and tofu pho 142
salt and pepper tofu 62
southern noodle soup 146
spiced tofu with aubergine and enoki mushrooms 66
stuffed courgette-flower salad with aubergine, peas and tofu 84
stuffed tomatoes with tofu, mushrooms and capers 68
tofu and tomatoes with spinach and basil 70
tofu knot 'chicken wings' 30
turmeric and dill tofu 128
vermicelli noodle salad bowls 137
watercress, ginger and silken tofu soup 157
winter melon stir-fry with tofu and glass noodles 104
**tomatoes**
egg and tomato noodle soup 151
egg and tomato scramble 52
lemongrass vegetable and pasta stew 134
mixed vegetable curry 56
orange, grilled peach and tomato salad 82
stuffed tomatoes with tofu, mushrooms and capers 68
sweet and sour cauliflower 46
sweet and sour tomato and golden beetroot soup 154
sweet and sour vegetable stir-fry 58
tofu and tomatoes with spinach and basil 70
**trifle**
fruity trifle 172
**turmeric**
king oyster mushroom and turmeric rice 130
turmeric and dill tofu 128

## V

vegan Vietnamese sausage 117
**vegetables**
any veg rice porridge 158
asparagus rice-noodle rolls with mushrooms and pumpkin 124
crispy vegetable crêpes 122
easy greens stir-fried with garlic 40
homemade vegetable stock 196
lemongrass noodle soup 148
lemongrass vegetable and pasta stew 134
mixed vegetable curry 56
mushroom and tofu pho 142
southern noodle soup 146
sweet and sour vegetable stir-fry 58
vegetable curry puffs 28
vegetable spring rolls 118
Vietnamese coffee ice cream 167
Vietnamese dough sticks 32

## W

**water chestnuts**
rainbow dessert 176
sweet potato and water chestnut wontons 27
water spinach with capers 43
**watercress**
watercress, ginger and silken tofu soup 157
watermelon and strawberry salad with chilli salt 78
watermelon and strawberry salad with chilli salt 78
winter melon stir-fry with tofu and glass noodles 104
**wontons**
sweet potato and water chestnut wontons 27
**wrappers**
dumpling wrappers 195

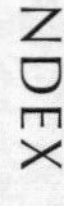

Published in 2023 by Hardie Grant Books,
an imprint of Hardie Grant Publishing

Hardie Grant Books (London)
5th & 6th Floors
52–54 Southwark Street
London SE1 1UN

Hardie Grant Books (Melbourne)
Building 1, 658 Church Street
Richmond, Victoria 3121

hardiegrantbooks.com



British Library Cataloguing-in-Publication Data.
A catalogue record for this book is available from the British Library.

Vietnamese Vegetarian
ISBN: 978-1-78488-551-9

10 9 8 7 6 5 4 3 2 1

Publishing Director: Kajal Mistry
Acting Publishing Director: Emma Hopkin
Senior Editor: Eila Purvis
Design & Art Direction: Evi-O.Studio | Susan Le
Illustrations: Evi-O.Studio | Susan Le, Emi Chiba & Kait Polkinghorne
Typesetting: Evi-O.Studio | Emi Chiba
Photographer: Uyen Luu
Photography assistant: Laurie Noble
Food stylists: Sam Dixon, Tamara Vos and Nga Le
Food stylist assistants: Lucy Turnbull and Florence Blair
Prop stylists: Louie Waller and Uyen Luu
Copy-editor: MiMi Aye
Proofreader: Suzanne Juby
Indexer: Cathy Heath
Production Controller: Martina Georgieva

Colour reproduction by p2d
Printed and bound in China by Leo Paper Products Ltd